Third Grade Language Ar

with Spelling, Reading, and Language Skills

Teacher's Manual *(Part 1)*
Lessons 1 to 80

Visit **McRuffy.com** for helpful resources to teach this curriculum!

Teacher's Manual *(Part 1)*
ISBN 978159269-3160

McRuffy Press Third Grade Language Arts Curriculum
ISBN 978159269-2118

Written and illustrated by
Brian Davis M. A. Ed.

Graphic Design by
Sherylynn Davis

McRuffy Press, LLC
P.O. Box 212
Raymore, MO 64083

816-331-7831

sales@mcruffy.com

www.McRuffy.com

Butterfly Spelling

Play a game on the back of the Spelling and Phonics workbook!

Move to spaces to collect the letters needed to spell words from the weekly spelling lists. Players can use a die, spinner, or draw numbers from a container to move around the board.

Players can start on any butterfly space on any flower. On other turns, players can move to a butterfly space and jump to any other another space and keep moving. For example, if a player is two spaces away from the butterfly and rolls a five, the player can move to that butterfly space and jump to another butterfly and move three more spaces.

If a player's playing piece is on a space, another player cannot move to the same space. The player must choose another direction to move. If the same letter is used more than once in a spelling word or spelling word list, the player must visit that space letter once for each time it is used.

Players will write the letters they capture to spell the words on a piece of paper or students can write the words first leaving space between letters so they may be circled as they are captured on the board.

Games: *Choose the rules for playing the game.*

Choose one:

Same Words Rule: All players race to spell the same spelling word.

Different Words Rule: Players choose different words from the spelling list. If a player chooses a word that has more letters than another player's word, the player with the longer word may automatically fill in enough letters so that both players are moving to get the same number of letters.

Choose one:

Letter Order Rule: Letters must by moved to in the order they are used in the words.

Letter Scramble Rule: Letters can be moved to in any order.

Choose the number of words: You may play a shorter game and only spell one word or a longer game and spell more words, such as a list of three words. You may write the words before the game with spaces between letters and then circle the letters as you move to them and land on them.

Go-Cart Games

Play games and race a go-cart on the back of the Language and Reading (LAR) workbook!

All games: In most games players answer a question or complete a task before earning a roll. Players will get a point for each correct answer or completed task. If a player lands on a space with a go-cart, players can complete a second task to roll again.

Players earn a point for each task completed successfully. Players also earn a point for being the first player to reach the FINISH space. Players may keep track of points using small objects such as counters, beans, or coins. Points can also be kept on paper as a scorecard. All players continue moving until they reach the FINISH space. The player with the most points wins.

Use a die, spinner, or draw numbers to move on the board with game pieces (small objects or game pawns).

Games (tasks to complete before moving)

Vocabulary Word Game 1: A teacher or another player reads a definition. The player says the vocabulary word. You may also include words from previous weeks.

Vocabulary Word Game 2: A teacher or another player reads a vocabulary word. The player says a definition. Players do not have to say the definitions exactly how it was presented in the curriculum. They just have to give a good explanation of the meaning. You may also include words from previous weeks.

Vocabulary Word Game 3: A teacher or another player reads a vocabulary word. The player taking the turn uses it in a sentence correctly.

Parts of Speech Game: Use a Reading Book with the story from the current week. Roll and move first. Find a word for the part of speech that is indicated on the space. If you land on a go-cart space, find any word and tell its part of speech.

Find A Word Sentence Game: Use a Reading Book with the story from the current week. One player or teacher reads a sentence from a page in the story. Tell the player the page number of the sentence. The player taking the turn has to find the sentence and point it out in the book. You could use a timer and put a time limit on finding the sentence.

Answer Sentence Game: Use a Reading Book with the story from the current week. Find a sentence on this page that tells __________.

Finish the Sentence Game: Use a Reading Book with the story from the current week. One player or the teacher reads part of a sentence. The player taking the turn finishes the sentence. You may tell the player the page the sentence is on or a choice of two pages. You could use a timer and put a time limit on finding the sentence.

Make up your own games, too!

From the back of the Writing Skills Workbook

Eight Great Writing Tips:

- **Practice regularly:** Writing, like any other skill, requires practice to improve. Keep a journal, create short stories, or write letters to family and friends.
- **Read widely:** Reading is an excellent way to improve writing skills. Read a variety of books, including fiction and non-fiction.
- **Brainstorm before writing:** Make a list of ideas before you start writing. This can include possible plot ideas, lists of facts, or even descriptions of characters.
- **Plan the structure of your writing:** Organize your writing into paragraphs and use transitional words and phrases to connect your ideas.
- **Use descriptive language:** Use descriptive language to create vivid images in the reader's mind. Use sensory details (sight, sound, taste, touch, and smell) to bring your writing to life.
- **Edit and revise:** Ask others to help you identify areas where they can improve, such as adding more details or correcting errors. Feel free to make changes. Writing is a process!
- **Share your work:** Share your writing with others, whether with family members or classmates. Ask for feedback on your writing.
- **Have fun:** Writing should be an enjoyable and creative process. You can experiment with different writing styles and genres. Write about things you are interested in or explore new ideas!

3rd Grade Language Arts

The McRuffy Press Third Phonics Language Arts continues the McRuffy Phonics and Reading series. The program is designed to build reading and language skills, review the phonetic and spelling structure of words, and incorporate handwriting into the process.

In this curriculum, there is less emphasis on teaching phonics skills. Most students will have mastered the basics of phonics after completing the other McRuffy Press levels. The phonics concepts will be reviewed and, more importantly, applied to more complex words.

Reading material is not as closely associated with the phonics concepts as in previous levels. The story structure is more sophisticated, with many more words and less re-reading. The child's phonetic knowledge is more naturally applied to any material that is read, so the purpose of the reading material is focused more on developing other reading skills such as comprehension skills, reading fluency, vocabulary development, and volition (an interest in reading).

An important part of the reading development involves the questions about the story that are found in the Teacher's Manual. Questions are constructed in several ways to reach different thinking levels: basic knowledge, application, synthesis, analysis, inference, and evaluation. Students are often asked to relate material to their own experiences. Asking students the make predictions about what happens next in the story requires students to synthesize facts from the story as well as their own knowledge to make a guess.

The lesson plan structure is the same as the other McRuffy Press levels. Lesson plans are broken into three sections: a numbered list of lesson objectives, a listing of materials used, and a teaching section with numbers that are correlated to the lesson objectives. In parentheses after each lesson objective is a letter that designates the main category the objective is teaching: P for Phonics, S for spelling, L for language, R for reading, H for handwriting, W for writing skills, and CW for creative writing.

Students will be given weekly spelling lists. The spelling words are based on the phonics concepts. Students will be given a pretest at the beginning of the week and a test at the end of the week.

Creative writing assignments are basically story starters. The teacher has the freedom to decide how much of the writing process is applied to the stories. You may want to have students write a few paragraphs or a few pages. Assignments can be completed in a single class session, or stories may be more fully developed over a number of days. You may set requirements for students to fully develop one story a quarter of their choosing. Writing may be kept in a writing journal.

Grammar and other language arts basics are taught and reviewed on a daily basis. Generally, the first lesson of the week has an emphasis on semantics (word structure) and vocabulary introduction, the next lesson focuses on syntax (sentence structure and grammar). The third lesson generally emphasizes higher level language skills such as analogies and categorizing. The fourth lesson features the creative writing assignment, and the last lesson deals more with larger text structure such as inference and main idea. Some variation of this structure does occur in the curriculum.

Handwriting assignments are given in the Lesson Plans. The sentences feature words from the vocabulary and spelling lists. Optional handwriting books give students prepared sheets that correspond to the Lesson Plans. The transitional handwriting books offer additional practice with cursive letter formation.

Please feel free to write us at: McRuffy Press P. O. Box 212, Raymore, MO 64083

Visit our website: www.mcruffy.com

e-mail: sales@mcruffy.com Phone 816-331-7831

Reference Section

Program Contents

1. Teacher's manual
2. Language and Reading workbook (abbreviated as LAR)
3. Spelling and Phonics workbook (abbreviated as SAP)
4. Writing Skills workbooks (abbreviated WSW)
5. Reading books
6. Handwriting Book (optional)
7. Resource Pack

Organization of the Teacher's Manual

The teacher's manual consists of:

1. Reference Section
2. Lesson plans

Lesson Plan Key

- Lesson objectives briefly state the concepts that are covered in the lesson. They answer the question: "What should the child be learning?" The objectives are numbered. The numbers correspond to the numbers in the teaching section. The letter at the end of each objective indicates what category the activity falls into.

    P = phonics, S = spelling, R = reading, L = language, CW = creative writing, W= writing skills, H = handwriting

- The preparation section lists any materials needed as well as any advance preparation needed to teach the lesson.

- The teaching section explains how to teach the lesson. Again, the numbers correspond with the numbers under lesson objectives. Some lessons are scripted. They have words in bold print that can be read directly to the students. It does not have to be followed exactly. Modify it if you would feel the child would understand better if things were said in a different way. You may have to elaborate more and check for understanding more.

Lesson Plans are organized into groups of five. Although this is to correspond to a school week, teachers should not hesitate to extend a lesson an extra day if that best fits the needs of the students. A school year consists of roughly 180 days. There are 160 days of lessons in this program. This will allow some flexibility for review, additional testing time, missed classes, etc.

Since each week introduces a new concept (except testing weeks) the program should be completed before moving on to the next program. For this reason, the program was designed to be slightly shorter than a school year.

Phonics Scope and Sequence

Lesson	Week	Concept
1	1	Blends with b, c, d, f
6	2	Blends with g, p, s, t
11	3	Long a
16	4	Long e
21	5	Long i
26	6	Long o
31	7	Long u
36	8	Review for Test 1
41	9	Short vowels
46	10	Vowel digraphs oo (both sounds) ow
51	11	Vowel digraphs ou, ow
56	12	Vowel digraph ea (different sounds)
61	13	Vowel digraphs and diphthongs oi, oy, oa
66	14	Vowel digraph ie, and sounds of y (long e and long i)
71	15	Consonant digraphs sh, th, ch, wh, ph
76	16	Review for Test 2
81	17	Three and four letter vowel sounds
86	18	Vowel + r
91	19	-air- sounds with various spellings
96	20	3-letter beginning blends: sch, thr, str, squ, spr, spl, shr, scr
101	21	Ending blends
106	22	Compound words
111	23	Broad o sound: au, ough, aw
116	24	Review for Test 3
121	25	Exceptions to rules
126	26	Silent Letters (beginning, medial, and ending)
131	27	Number prefixes (such as bi-, tri-, etc.)
136	28	Hard and Soft g and c
141	29	Words ending with the suffix -able
146	30	Words ending with the suffixes –ful and -less
151	31	Finding root words in multi-syllable words
156	32	Review for Test 4

Language Scope and Sequence

Lesson

1. Vocabulary Development
2. Grammar
3. Poems, -ly suffixes
4. Contractions, Creative Writing
5. Comprehension
6. Plurals
7. Nouns and Verbs
8. Singular or Plural Nouns
9. Creative Writing
10. Interpret a Graph
11. Synonyms
12. Pronouns
13. Nouns and Pronouns
14. Creative Writing
15. Story Order
16. Antonyms
17. Adjectives
18. Add Adverbs to sent.
19. Creative Writing
20. Cause and Effect
21. Suffixes ing and ed
22. Adjectives
23. Present & Past Tense
24. Creative Writing
25. Following Directions
26. Dictionary Skills
27. Irregular Nouns
28. Kinds of Sentences . ! ?
29. Creative Writing
30. Recalling Details
31. Homophones
32. Helping Verbs
33. Scrambled Sentences
34. Creative Writing
35. Inferences

36-40 Review and Test 1

41. Classifying Words
42. Prepositions
43. Fact vs. Opinion
44. Creative Writing
45. Main Idea
46. Prefixes un & re
47. Plural Nouns
48. Categories
49. Creative Writing
50. Combining Sentences
51. Dictionary Skills
52. Tense: present, past, and future
53. Analogies
54. Creative Writing
55. Figurative Language
56. Homophones
57. Nouns or Verbs by Context
58. Paragraphs
59. Creative Writing
60. Recalling Details
61. Prefix: pre-
62. Subject Part of a Sentence
63. Completing Sentences (Cloze)
64. Creative Writing
65. Adding Details
66. Categories
67. Predicate Part of a Sentence
68. Similes
69. Creative Writing
70. Inference
71. Analogies
72. Subject and Predicate Parts
73. Matching Subjects to Predicates
74. Creative Writing
75. Compare and Contrast

76-80 Review and Test 2

81. Semantic Map
82. Predicate Adjectives
83. Add Adj. And Adv. to Sentences
84. Creative Writing
86. Prefix - over
87. Cloze activity
88. Analogies
89. Creative Writing
90. Note-taking (Outlining)
91. Distinguishing their, there, and they're
92. Prepositions (rev.)
93. Questions: The Five W's

Language Scope and Sequence

94. Creative Writing
95. Graphic Organizer
96. Analogies
97. Possessive Pronouns
98. Combining Sentences
99. Creative Writing
100. Paraphrasing
101. Synonyms or Antonyms
102. Articles: a, an, the
103. Choosing a & an
104. Creative Writing
105. Drawing conclusions - inference
106. Categories
107. Irregular Verbs
108. Types of sentences
109. Creative Writing
110. Note-taking (rev.)
111. ABC order to any letter
112. Proper Nouns: titles and history
113. Parts of speech
114. Creative Writing
115. Fact vs. Opinion
116-120 Review and Test 3
121. Helping verbs
122 Commonly Confused Words: to, its, there, your
123. Analogies
124. Creative Writing
125. Cause and Effect
126. Single syllable comparative adjectives & adverbs
127. Subject-Verb Agreement
128. Two-syllable comparative adjectives & adverbs
129. Creative Writing
130. Compare and Contrast
131. Review parts of speech
132. Linking Verbs
133. Facts vs. Opinions
134. Creative Writing
135. Graphic Organizer
136. Review subject and predicate
137. Change . to ?'s (word order)
138. Sentences and the 5 Senses
139. Creative Writing
140. Writing Directions
141. Analogies
142. Adding nouns to sentences
143. Categories
144. Creative Writing
145. Using a variety of ways to name a subject in a paragraph
146. Cause and effect
147. Subject and Predicate, adjectives review
148. Review prepositions
149. Creative Writing
150. Finding the main idea
151. Similes
152. Parts of Speech – All
153. Analogies
154. Creative Writing
155. Story Sequence
156-160 Review and Test 4

Spelling Program

In addition to the spelling activities in the Spelling and Phonics book you may want to establish a weekly spelling routine. A suggested routine is detailed below based on a weekly plan of five lessons.

Day 1 (lessons ending with 1 or 6) Spelling Pre-test. Give the spelling words as dictation. Have students check and correct any words that are wrong.

Discuss any unknown words. Ask students if there are any words they don't know. Make up short definitions or have students find the words in the dictionary.

Day 2 (lessons ending with 2 or 7) Oral spelling: Spell the first half of the list orally.

Day 3 (lessons ending with 3 or 8) Oral spelling: Spell the second half of the list orally.

Day 4 (lessons ending with 4 or 9) Sentence Dictation: use sentences from activities or make up new sentences. Not all the spelling words need to be used in sentences. You may also have students spell any of the words missed in the Day 1 pre-test.

Some words may appear in more than one week to emphasize a different spelling theme.

Spelling Lists

Beginning Lesson

1 crowd, frighten, blueberries, dresser, brief, closet, flour, creature, drenched, fly, frame, branch, fruit, blanket, clump

6 glue, photograph, fireplace, pray, scout, skinny, asleep, smudge, snowflake, respect, instead, swiftly, control, twinkle

11 toothpaste, tray, osprey, raindrop, layer, repaid, straight, steak, reign, great, weight, they, celebrate, nation, remain

16 alive, entire, ivory, midnight, pliers, provide, realize, satisfy, scientist, silent, skyrocket, terrify, title, iceberg, child, kindness

21 tornado, snowstorm, explode, gross, location, overflow, avocado, poem, echo, doughnut, hotel, raincoat, automobile, toaster, toenails, wheelbarrow

26 understood, bookmark, footstool, mongoose, cartoon, bloodhound, mood, bamboo, doorknob, flood, goodnight, kangaroo, moonlight, poodle, school, woodpecker

31 between, speech, weekend, teaspoon, disappear, teacher, reason, piece, shield, turkey, money, family, forty, grumpy, everything, fourteen

36 Review List: frighten, drenched, blanket, photograph, instead, celebration, toothpaste, disappear, everything, recognize, scientist, automobile, doughnut, understood, moonlight, bloodhound

41 wagon, lemon, object, spinach, music, astonish, rather, adventure, giant, rectangle, insect, amusement, hungry, cactus, number

46 nephew, review, newspaper, avenue, continue, rescue, shoestring, canoe, through, caribou, tourist, youth, costume, include, student

51 mountain, thousand, counter, cloudy, amount, announce, couch, powder, coward, shower, cowboy, brownie, downpour, eyebrow, flour, flower

56 teacher, increase, season, meaning, beagle, pleasant, meadow, forehead, treasure, breakfast, beautiful, steak, earthworm, search

61 toaster, loyalty, sirloin, voyage, approach, oyster, rowboat, rejoice, toadstool, moisture, porpoise, employ, avoid, cowboy

66 achieve, magnify, pies, motorcycle, ability, believe, multiplied, windshield, everything, butterflies, why, movies, shriek, country

71 orchard, sandwich, Christmas, parachute, alphabet, paragraph, sunshine, shrub, shadow, together, thanksgiving, theater, leather, whenever, whisper, somewhere

76 Review List: adventure, rectangle, continue, nephew, shoestring, mountain, eyebrow, breakfast, teacher, approach, toaster, rejoice, avoid, windshield, butterflies, country, parachute, whisper, alphabet, shadow

Spelling Lists

81 thoughtful, mighty, righteous, daughter, taught, doughnut, eighteen, throughout, enough, caught, frighten, cough, laugh, lightweight

86 hamburger, direction, overboard, overheard, overturn, squirm, forgive, curious, surrender, earthworm, lumberyard, murmur, certain, partner

91 parent, wear, America, charity, embarrass, sheriff, terrible, dictionary, arrow, character, library, chair, their, where

96 throat, schooner, squabble, scrounge, stranger, shrivel, splinter, shrubbery, sprinkle, sprout, squash, schedule, screwdriver, strawberries, splurge, thread

101 watchdog, hopscotch, scratch, misjudge, hedgehog, bridge, exchange, endanger, rearrange, wasteful, tasty, pastry, whistle, castle, wrestle

106 underneath, afternoon, breakfast, briefcase, waterfall, otherwise, meanwhile, everything, lightweight, nationwide

111 lawnmower, auction, sawhorse, because, automobile, astronaut, awkward, crawl, faucet, exhausted, bought, thoughtless, sought, fought

116 Review: daughter, frighten, cough, hamburger, curious, lumberyard, dictionary, embarrass, library, splinter, screwdriver, throat, watchdog, exchange, whistle, afternoon, lightweight, everything, because, bought

121 leopard, recipe, building, friendship, against, floodlight, sew, sweetheart, movement, someone, liver, honey

126 weightless, knuckle, tongue, plumber, sketch, wrapper, handsome, knowledge, design, island, rhyme, muscle, spaghetti, half, iron

131 binocular, centimeter, decimal, hexagon, octopus, quarterly, unicycle, century, tripod, pentagon, quadruple, millimeter, polygon, heptagon, nonagon

136 message, bicycle, region, official, genius, succeed, gentle, strategy, reduce, suggestion, accident, geography, chance, science, giant

141 changeable, disposable, squeezable, comfortable, replaceable, manageable, enjoyable, remarkable, fixable, unbelievable, stretchable, questionable, unreasonable, noticeable, portable

146 speechless, useless, thoughtless, painful, plentiful, penniless, joyful, priceless, skillful, rightful, suspenseful, colorful, needless, sugarless, powerful

151 capitalize, discovery, dangerous, possibilities, precaution, favorite, invention, alphabetize, excellent, children, unlimited, measurements, construction, neighborhood, electricity

156 Review: building, leopard, tongue, island, octopus, century, quadruple, science, genius, suggestion, comfortable, enjoyable, unbelievable, noticeable, priceless, colorful, plentiful, dangerous, invention, electricity

Reading Book List

Lesson	Story
Book 1	
1	A Tune For Tess
6	Matt's Birthday Blessing: The New Bike
11	Matt's Birthday Blessing: Happy Birthday
16	The Wrong Goal
21	One Is Enough: Part 1
26	One is Enough: Part 2
31	My Shoes Got the Blues: Like Layers of an Onion
36	Test 1 Review: No story
41	My Shoes Got the Blues: The Sky's the Limit
46	My Shoes Got the Blues: Sole Winning
51	Tidbit and the Bell
56	Tidbit to the Rescue
61	Fritz and the Fire
66	Bobcat Cowboys on Trial: Part 1
71	Bobcat Cowboys on Trial: Part 2
76	Bobcat Cowboys on Trial: Part 3
Book 2	
81	The Underground Railroad (article in LAR workbook)
82	Elijah's Coming: Part 1
86	Elijah's Coming: Part 2
91	Elijah's Coming: Part 3
96	Matthew and Goliath: Chapters 1 to 5
101	Matthew and Goliath: Chapters 6 to 9
106	Bobcat Cowboys Steal the Show: Part 1
111	Bobcat Cowboys Steal the Show: Part 2
116	Bobcat Cowboys Steal the Show: Part 3
121	The King is Coming
126	Big Tom's Café
131	Pigs in the Pancakes
136	The Case of the Missing Trumpeter
141	The Case of the Missing Trumpeter
146	Bobcat Cowboys Take the Cake: Part 1
151	Bobcat Cowboys Take the Cake: Part 2
156	Test 4 Review: No story

Reading Vocabulary List

1 A Tune For Tess: Consequences, comfortable, eavesdrop, expression, favorite, handkerchief, hopeless, minute, tough, trough,

6 Matt's Birthday Blessing, The New Bike: awesome, cafe, enough, explanation, garage, miracle, mountain, obedient, quoted

11 Matt's Birthday Blessing, Happy Birthday: envelope, embarrassed, disciplined

16 The Wrong Goal: laboratory, explosion, customer, occasionally, millionaire, invention, ordinary, identification, artificial

21 One Is Enough part 1: Christmas, companies, cousin, curiosity, different, disappointed, electricity, machine

26 One Is Enough part 2: attention, recognized, underneath, warehouse

31 My Shoes Got the Blues: Like Layer of an Onion: none

36 Test 1 Review List: consequences, eavesdrop, cafe, obedient, embarrassed, envelope, laboratory, invention, artificial, curiosity, disappointed, attention, recognized, cousin

41 My Shoes Got the Blues: The Sky's The Limit: advertisement, allowance, autograph, contestant, decision, distracted, idol, imaginary, jealous, nervous, secretary

46 My Shoes Got the Blues: Sole Winning: ordinarily, important, stopwatch, responsible, immediately, determined, impossible

51 Tidbit and the Bell: adventure, attention, commotion, complain, creature, daydream, encourage, introduced, refreshing, tremendous, trustworthy

56 Tidbit to the Rescue: concerned, desperately, expand, explain, relief, unexpected

61 Fritz and the Fire: confident, dangerous, hospitality, instructed, suspected, innocent

66 Bobcat Cowboys On Trial part 1: hippopotamus, porcupine, prosecuting, stenograph

71 Bobcat Cowboys On Trial part 2: customer, disturbing, dreadful, opossum, panicking, serious

76 Bobcat Cowboys On Trial part 3: allergic, business, concerned, handsome, mathematical, theatre

Test 2 Review List: imaginary, creature, explain, dangerous, porcupine, serious

Reading Vocabulary List

82 Elijah's Coming, part 1: blacksmith, encourage, distance, continue, underground, mistreat, conductor

86 Elijah's Coming, part 2: accident, curious, disguise, miracle, protection

91 Elijah's Coming, part 3: biscuits, decision, identify, instructions, plantation

96 Matthew and Goliath, Chapters 1 to 5: Compassion, distracting, inexpensive, murmur, nervous, opportunity, persecute

101 Matthew and Goliath, Chapters 6 to 10: Frustrated, choir, expressions, expected, attention, recognized, auditorium, assembly

106 Bobcat Cowboys Steal the Show, part 1: Brainstorm, otherwise, meanwhile, tournament, expected, decorations

111 Bobcat Cowboys Steal the Show, part 2: lawnmower, auction, sawhorse, because, automobile, astronaut, awkward, crawl, faucet, exhausted

116 Test 3 Review List: encourage, accident, identify, recognize, opportunity, expect, tournament, exhausted, distracting, auditorium

121 The King Is Coming: carriage, cobbler, noblemen, tailor, guard

126 Big Tom's Café: café, constantly, customer, impression, restaurant

131 Pigs in the Pancakes: Combination, dickering, inspector, invested, livestock, professional

136 The Case of the Missing Trumpeter, part 1: cautiously, daffodil, feline, ferocious, incubation, predator

141 The Case of the Missing Trumpeter, part 2: cygnets, delightful, distracting, undercover

146 The Bobcat Cowboys Take the Cake, part 1: appetizer, bridle, corral, mutton, notorious

151 The Bobcat Cowboys Take the Cake, part 2: concentrate, evidence, reception

156 Test 4 Review List: appetizer, carriage, concentrate, constantly, customer, cygnets, delightful, ferocious, notorious, predator

The Writing Process

The McRuffy Press writing skills program

The McRuffy Press writing skills program underwent a major change in the spring of 2018. The program now includes the Writing Skills Workbook. The workbook further the develops the writing program and aligns it with current national standards. Previous writing assignments are still included in the previous form. This includes activities that are still in the Language and Reading (LAR) workbook and creative writing assignments on the fourth lesson of each week. The creative writing assigments can fit the process outlined below. Except for testing weeks, most weeks have two more writing assignments that are found in the Writing Skills Workbook.

The Writing/Publishing process may use the following steps:

The full writing process can involve many steps. Again, you do not have to have students do every step for every assignment. At the beginning of the year, students may only write three or four paragraphs. Stories do not have to be long. They don't have to be complex. Students will evolve into better writers with practice.

Some steps in the writing process may be too tedious every week. If so, skip or adapt those steps by giving additional guidance or help. Creating a story should make the student feel empowered. It should be an experience for students that builds confidence. Children should learn to express themselves in new ways. Keep the process positive and fun, not overwhelming.

Brain Storming: In this step, consider any and all ideas. Hopefully some of the ideas in the creative writing assignments will help begin this process. Make brief notes about any ideas that are brought up in this process. The notes can be one or two words or a short sentence. Using a chalkboard or white dry erase board (white board) is a good idea.

Pre-Writing: In this step the student should choose the idea and begin to organize and develop thoughts more completely.

Organize: Make into a graphic organizer. See Language and Reading workbook pages 77 and 126 for examples. Organize around a synopsis (brief description of the story idea). Characters, setting, chain of events, or other story elements.

Write: Write the rough draft. This may be the final step for several of the assignments that you do not want to take to the publishing phase.

Processing: In this steps student are given critical feedback for their story. This can come from the teacher or other students. Students giving feedback should be instructed to do so in a helpful and thoughtful way. The idea should be to make the story better. This may include asking the author to clarify things they didn't understand. Students may also have ideas for adding to the story. Students receiving the feedback should be instructed in being open to receive the ideas of others. It shouldn't be a threatening process.

Students should be encouraged to consider the opinions of others, but they do not necessarily have to make changes they don't want to. The processing step is very good for developing language and communication skills and analytical skills. In a homeschool setting, parents may want to get students together with other students outside their families for this step.

Edit: Students may rewrite any portion of the story that changes from the processing step. This can be done by marking out sections and penciling in the changes.

Technical changes: The student, then the teacher should evaluate the material for any technical mistakes such as spelling, punctuation, and grammar.

Rewrite: Copy the material with all the changes.

Proof: Check the rewritten material for any new mistakes. The student and the teacher may be involved in this.

Illustrate: Plan the pictures. Think about what to illustrate. Students should understand that not every idea in a story could or should be illustrated. The pictures are like snapshots of the action. Have students look at other books such as the book in the reading assignment and see what part of the text is illustrated and what isn't.

When the stories were developed for the curriculum, the text was broken into sections by length (approximate number of words). From that section of text, a decision was made about illustrating. What one thing could be illustrated from that page?

You may want students to make the pictures as line drawings, like the pictures in the reading books of the curriculum. This would allow them to be photocopied more easily. Students could then color the photocopies if they would like.

Publish: Put the story in a book form that can be shared with others. Again, this may be a single copy or it may be photocopied. If you plan on photocopying, put only one staple in the books while the students are creating them. Have the students number the pages. Take the staple back out to copy, then staple it again. You may also want students to use plain white paper for the cover instead of colored paper or construction paper if the cover is to be copied also.

The following two steps go beyond the publishing process. These two steps develop language skills to an even higher level. Not every work will be suitable for these steps, but they can be quite enjoyable for the students.

Playwright: Think of the story in terms of a play. How might the story be performed? What dialog would you use? When a book is adapted for a movie or play, it is changed to make it more presentable to an audience. For example, a character's thoughts have to be transformed to action or dialog for the audience to understand. This again is a brainstorming and writing process.

Perform: Perform a play adapted from the child's story. Maybe a single child will perform every part, maybe other children will be involved. Students may make costumes, props, and scenery as a part of the process. The plays may be video taped so students can see their own performances.

Lesson 1

Lesson Objectives

1. Students will spell fifteen words correctly. (S & P)
2. Students will blend initial consonants b, c, d, and f. (L)
3. Students will learn vocabulary words. (L)
4. Students will begin reading the story *A Tune For Tess*. (R)
5. Students will copy sentences neatly and correctly. (H)

Materials

LAR workbook pages 3 and 4
SAP workbook page 5
Book: *A Tune For Tess*

Teaching

1. Write each blend. (bl, br, cl, cr, dr, fl, fr) **Tell me a word that begins with b-l.** Repeat for the other six blends.

   Use SAP workbook page 5. **Look at the words in the pink box. They all begin with two letter consonant blends. Read the words.**

   Complete the workbook page in three parts. **Alphabetize the words on the numbered lines. Number the words in the list first, so it will be easy to correct if you get a word out of order.** Next, **Write all the beginning blends used in the spelling words on the short lines.** Conclude the lesson, **Use any four of the blends and write another word that is not on the spelling list that begins with that blend.**

   Spelling list: crowd, frighten, blueberries, dresser, brief, closet, flour, creature, drenched, fly, frame, branch, fruit, blanket, clump

2. Students will complete the crossword puzzle on LAR workbook page 3 using words that begin with these blends. Students will be given a clue.

3. Introduce vocabulary words for the story, *A Tune For Tess*. The list is printed on the title page of the book. Students will be introduced to the meanings of the words on LAR workbook page 4.

   This sheet is a teaching sheet that does not have an exercise for the students to complete. Students will read the words using the phonetic spelling after it, if necessary. Definitions and example sentences follow the phonetic spellings.

   The phonetic spellings are used as pronunciation guides. They do not use the same symbols found in dictionaries, but rather standard letters. For this reason, some liberties have been taken, especially with the schwa sounds on this page and others like it in the curriculum. The pronunciations are not always 100% accurate, but are intended to help students read the words.

   Vocabulary list: Consequences, comfortable, eavesdrop, expression, favorite, handkerchief, hopeless, minute, tough, trough.

4. Students will begin reading the first chapter of *A Tune For Tess*. Introduce the story. Have students look at the title page. Students should read the title, the description on the title page, and the vocabulary words.

   This story is set in the early 1900's. Look for things in the story that let us know that it happened a long time ago.

5. Use the handwriting sheet or have the children write the following sentences:

   We need flour to make blueberry muffins.
   The dresser is next to the closet.

SAP Page 5
Spelling List
Alphabetized

	1. drenched	1. blanket
	2. dresser	2. blueberries
	3. flour	3. branch
	4. fly	4. brief
	5. frame	5. closet
	6. frighten	6. clump
	7. fruit	7. creature
		8. crowd

Blends: bl, br, cl, cr, dr, fl, fr

LAR Page 3

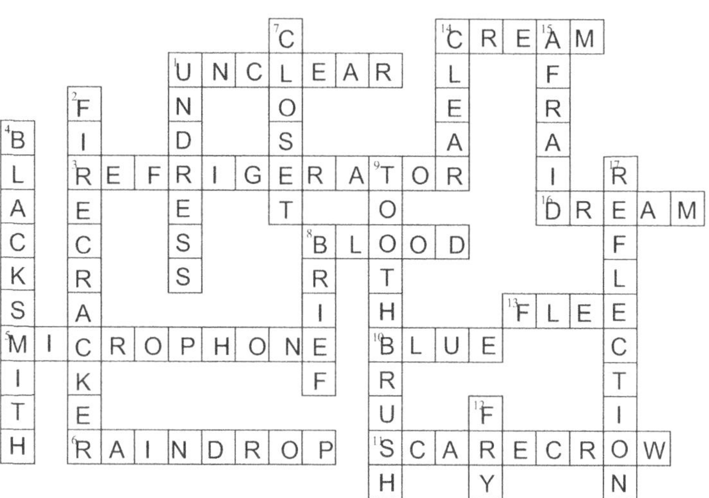

Lesson 2

Lesson Objectives

1. Students will write spelling words. (S)
2. Students will complete analogies with spelling words. (S & L)
3. Students will correct sentences by completing blends. (L)
4. Students will read the story *A Tune For Tess*. (R)
5. Students will copy sentences neatly and correctly. (H)
6. Students will write a narrative. (W)

Materials

SAP Workbook page 6
LAR Workbook page 5
WSW pages 4 and 5
Book: *A Tune For Tess*

Teaching

1. Write the word *frozen*. **I can use the letters in this word to make other words. I can use the z-o-n-e to spell *zone*. Do you see other words that can be spelled with the letters in *frozen*?** (for, one, or, ore, fro, fern, etc.)

   Repeat with the word *bridge*. (possibilities include bride, ride, rid, big, beg, bird, red, rig, big, bed, bid, grid)

   Next write the words bread, fresh, and clear. Next, write the words her, red, and lace. **Look at the last three words. Read them.** (her, red, lace) **What word from the first list has all the letters used to spell *her*?** (fresh) Repeat for red (bread) and lace (clear).

   Top of SAP Workbook page 6: **Small words are next to sets of lines. The words were made using letters from spelling words. The list is in the middle of the page. Match the spelling word that has the letters to make the words next to the lines. Write the spelling word on the lines next to the word that can be made from it.**

2. Use the bottom of SAP workbook page 6. **On the bottom section of the workbook page are analogies. Analogies compare two sets of words. The first two words are alike in some way. The way they are alike is similar in some way to the other pair of words.**

   Let's look at the first one. Brow is to brown as crow is to *blank*. What spelling word is like the word *crow*? (crowd) **Write the word *crowd* on the first set of lines. How did we change the word rip to make the word *grip*?** (We added a letter to it.) **When you add a letter to the end of *brow*, you get the word *brown*. When you added a letter to *crow* you made the word *crowd*. Complete the other four analogies.**

3. Write the words bend, gain, finch, bat, and cane. Have the students read the words. Next, have the students add l or r after the initial consonant to make new words.

   LAR Workbook page 5: **Proofread the sentences for words with missing blends. Write the sentences correctly.**

4. Have students finish reading the first chapter of *A Tune For Tess* and/or begin chapter 2. Ask questions about chapter 1:

   What was Old Tess? (a mule)
   What did Momma want to make from the flour sack? (a dress for Addie)
   Why was Papa excited about the new mule? (It could work faster.)
   What book did Papa like to read? (the Bible)
   Why couldn't the family keep two mules? (They couldn't afford to feed both.)
   What does eavesdrop mean? (listen when you're not supposed to)
   What did Papa mean when he said he might have to put Old Tess down? (shoot her)
   How would you feel about that if you were the child in the story?
   What might you try to do to solve the problem?

5. Use the handwriting sheet or have the children write the following sentences:

   The crab clung fiercely to the rock.
   We quickly picked the fruit from the branches.

6. There are two pages in this activity. The first page is a chart of words that give order in writing. Discuss the page with students. **Certain words help the reader know the order of events when they read your writing. Words based on numbers like first, second, and third are a clear way to give order. Often the last step will be a word such as "finally" to indicate that there are no more steps. Tell me the steps you would use to brush your teeth using number words. Other words help give a timeframe or order. Look at the list. Tell me some sentences using these words.**

   Write a narrative about making blueberry pancakes from fresh picked blueberries on the second page. Students will use words that indicate order. Steps are suggested. Students do not have to include all steps in the story. Students should use at least 3 spelling words and 1 vocabulary word.

Answers SAP page 6

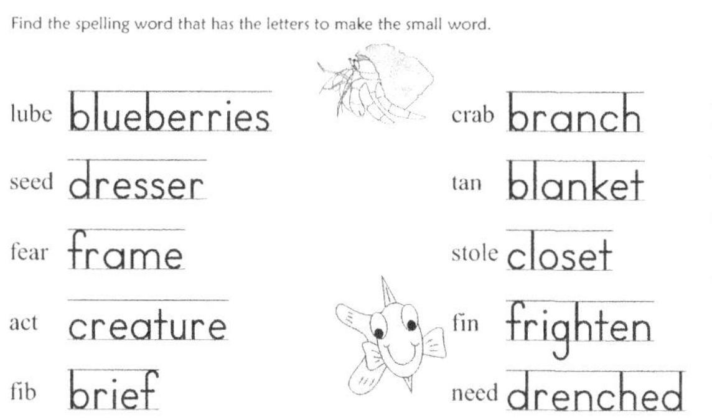
Find the spelling word that has the letters to make the small word.

lube	blueberries	crab	branch
seed	dresser	tan	blanket
fear	frame	stole	closet
act	creature	fin	frighten
fib	brief	need	drenched

crowd frighten blueberries dresser brief closet flour
creature drenched fly frame branch fruit blanket clump

Write spelling words on the lines to make analogies.

1. brow is to **brown** as **crow** is to crowd
2. damp is to **dump** as **clamp** is to clump
3. [illegible] flour
4. dog is to **pet** as **apple** is to fruit
5. blew is to **blow** as **flew** is to fly

Answers LAR page 5

1. The **bright flashlight blinded** the **bullfrog**.
2. Mom **dreaded cleaning** the **refrigerator**.
3. A **blanket** is in the **closet**.
4. **Grandmother** will **drink** the **glass** of **grapefruit** juice.
5. A fuzzy **creature** is **creeping across** the **floor**.

Lesson 3

Lesson Objectives

1. Students will read poems. (L & R)
2. Students will review the spelling words. (S)
3. Students will add the suffix -ly to words. (L & S)
4. Students will read part of the story *A Tune For Tess*. (R)
5. Students will copy sentences neatly and correctly. (H)

Materials

LAR Workbook page 6
SAP Workbook page 7
Book: *A Tune For Tess*
Notebook for a writing journal

Teaching

1. Have students turn to LAR workbook page 6. Introduce a quatrain poem to students. Poems are reprinted on the next page. **Poems are arranged in sets of lines called stanzas. Poems with four line stanzas are called quatrains. Some quatrain poems have only four lines, others have several stanzas. Most quatrains follow a rhyming pattern. The last word in each line rhymes with the last word in another line. Read at the poem *Bright Lights.* The first two lines rhyme and the last two words rhyme. What is the rhyming pattern for *Blueberry*?** (ABAB or 1st and 3rd lines rhyme, 2nd and 4th lines rhyme)

   The following paragraph is also printed in the workbook. ***Crayfish* does not have a rhyming pattern. It does feature alliteration. Crayfish, crawls, and creek all begin with the same sound. Using words that begin with the same sound is called *alliteration*. What other examples of alliteration are in the poem?**

   Can you write a quatrain poem? Think of ideas you might like to write about. Make a list. Maybe you can write a poem about an observation, like *Bright Lights.* Maybe you can write about something you enjoy, like the poem *Blueberry.*

   The poem *Crayfish* describes what life might be like for a small animal avoiding predators. We might enjoy watching ducks drift in the water. The poem gives us a different way of looking at it. Maybe you can think of an unusual way of looking at something.

   Allow students time to brainstorm ideas and write them. Students will be given more poetry writing instruction in lesson 4 and other lessons. A poem about doing a chore will be developed as an example in future lessons.

2. Use SAP workbook page 7. Have students complete the sentences with spelling words.

3. Write the words *live, swift, sudden, mournful, eager, hopeful.* Tell the students that you want to add a suffix to each of these words. Ask students if they can tell you a definition for the word suffix. (letters added to the end of words) Also review the term *root word.* (the word before a suffix was added)

   Use a piece of paper. Have students number down the side from 1 to 6. Ask students to add the suffix –ly to each of the words from the list and write the new words on the lines.

   (Continued on the next page)

Next, read the sentences to the students: The bird is quick. The bird flies quickly.

Ask what is quick in the first sentence. (the bird) Ask what the word *quickly* refers to in the second sentence. (the way the bird flies)

Say: **When ly is added to words, most of the time they become adverbs. Remember, adverbs tell more about verbs. In the example sentence, the word *quickly* tells us more about the word flies.**

Have students look at the book, *A Tune For Tess*. Each of the words that the students added the ly suffix to can be found in the first chapter of the book. Have students write the verbs that the adverbs describe along with the page number (optional: give students the page numbers). Answers: Lively page 4 movin' and/or moved. Swiftly page 4 ran. Suddenly page 4 felt. Mournfully page 5 bray. Eagerly page 5 nodded. Hopefully, page 6 asked.

4. Finish reading the second chapter of *A Tune For Tess*. Ask the students the following questions, then read chapter 3.

   Why did the boy leave home? (He was looking for someone that wanted Tess.)

   What does "stretch a penny" mean? (to buy more with less money)

   Find the word "expression" on pages 9 and 12. Does expression mean the same in each sentence? (On page 9, the word expression means showing an emotion by the way someone looks. Page 12 shows a different way to tell a thought in the sentence.)

   Was Mr. Lucas an honest man? What are some things in the chapter that let you know this? (He wanted to pay for Old Tess. He wanted to make sure it was all right with the boy's father.)

   What's another name for the instrument called a fiddle? (violin)

5. Use the handwriting sheet or have the children write the following sentences:

   The pink blanket is in the closet. The furry creature frightened me.

Answers SAP page 7

1. Chickens can only **fly** a **brief** time.
2. The blue **fruits** are **blueberries**.
3. I didn't mean to **frighten** the little **creature**.
4. The rain **drenched** the **crowd** of people.
5. I keep my clothes in the **dresser** and the **closet**. (or closet, dresser)
6. We tossed the **blankets** over a **frame** to dry.
7. The **flour** made a **clump** of dough.
8. The squirrel jumped onto the **branch**.

Quatrain Poems LAR page 6

Bright Light
The moth was drawn to the light
It tried to stop with all its might
but the glow just pulled it in
and soon it started sizzlin'

Blueberry
Blueberry is my favorite pie
With filling round and blue
I'm sure if you will only try
You'll find you like it too

Crayfish
The crayfish crawls in a creek
Fleeing flocks of floating ducks
Blended in, a small brown blob
With dreaded drakes drifting by

Lesson 4

Lesson Objectives

1. Students will review contractions. (S)
2. Students will read the story *A Tune For Tess*. (R)
3. Students will continue developing a poem. (CW)
4. Students will copy sentences neatly and correctly. (H)

Materials

SAP Workbook page 8
Book: *A Tune For Tess*
Writing Journal

Teaching

1. Review the term contraction. It's when we put two words together. Write the words **would not** and **wouldn't**. Point to the apostrophe. Ask students if they can remember the name of this punctuation mark. Ask what it does in the word **wouldn't**. (It shows that letters were taken out.) Ask what letters were left out when we turned **would not** into the contraction **wouldn't**.

   Review a few contractions, such as: I'm, can't, they're. Ask students to find the words that make up the contractions. (I am, cannot, they are).

   SAP workbook page 8: **Read the sentences. Find the words that can form contractions. Write the contractions on the lines.**

2. Ask questions about chapter 3.

   Who in the family knew how to play the fiddle? (Papa)

   How did the boy know he was in trouble when he saw his father? (by the expression on his father's face)
   What did the boy write the note on? (a chalkboard)
   What happened to the note? (His sister erased it.)
   What did Papa ask his son to give him? (a quarter)
   Where do you think Papa is going at the end of chapter 3?

   Students will now read chapter four of the book *A Tune For Tess*.

3. Use the poetry idea list developed in lesson 3. Start by free writing. **Pick an idea. Simply write about it. Just get different thoughts and possibilities written down. It doesn't have to rhyme or fit any kind of a pattern at this time. It doesn't have to be a poem yet.**

   Here's an example of a poem idea about a chore. This is the free writing part. It doesn't look or sound like a poem yet.

   I need to mow the lawn, but it's so hot outside. The mower is in the shed. It's messy and dark in the shed. Sometimes the mower is hard to start. If I were grass I don't think I would like to be mowed.

   Students will add more to their poems in lesson 5.

4. Use the handwriting sheet or have the children write the following sentences:

   The rain drenched the crowd. The chef quickly added the flour.

Answers SAP page 4

don't
wasn't
They're
I'm
isn't
She'll
That's
couldn't
It's or isn't
aren't
couldn't
We'll
They'll
wouldn't

Lesson Objectives

1. Students will answer questions about the story *A Tune For Tess*. (L)
2. Students will take a spelling test. (S)
3. Students will refine creative writing. (CW)
4. Students will copy a sentence neatly and correctly. (H)

Materials

Creative writing assignment from Lesson 4
LAR Workbook

Teaching

1. Use LAR workbook page 7. Answer the questions about the story.
2. Have students number their paper from 1 to 15. Give the following words as dictation.

   1. closet, 2. fly, 3. frighten, 4. blanket, 5. flour, 6. frame, 7. dresser, 8. brief, 9. drenched, 10. branch, 11. blueberries, 12. creature, 13. fruit, 14. crowd, 15. clump
3. Use the writing from lesson 4. **Look at what you wrote in the last lesson. Begin to think of what you wrote in terms of a poem. Poems use few words to express ideas. Look for possible rhyming words or maybe alliteration. Edit your writing by taking out necessary words. Make a list of possible rhyming words or words that begin with the same sound that might fit your poem idea.**

   Look at the example on the workbook page. This is the example I read in the last lesson. Notes have been added. Find the example of alliteration. (dusty, dumpy, dark, dingy)

   There are also notes on possible rhymes. Think of words that might come at the ending of a line. After making a list of rhymes, you may see words that fit the idea that you are writing about. What are some rhyming ideas in the example? (hot: not, lot, bought, caught. Shed: red, bed, dread, fed, led, head, said, wed.) **Other words could have been rhymed, so you may add to your notes later if an idea doesn't work out.**
4. Use the handwriting sheet or have the children write the following sentences:

   The papers were in the briefcase.

   We saw a flock of geese flying.

LAR Workbook Answers

1. C 2. C
3. B 4. A
5. A 6. B
7. C. Papa Plays a Tune

Lesson 6

Lesson Objectives

1. Students will review consonant blends with g, p, s, and t. (S & P)
2. Students will learn vocabulary words for *The New Bike.* (L)
3. Students will begin reading the story *The New Bike.* (R)
4. Students will copy sentences neatly and correctly. (H)

Materials

SAP Workbook page 9
LAR Workbook page 8
Book: *Matt's Birthday Blessing: The New Bike*

Teaching

1. Write each blend. (gl, gr, pl, pr, sc, sk, sl, sm, sn, sp, st, sw, tr, tw) Have students think of words that begin with the blends.

   Use SAP workbook page 9. **Find the spelling word that matches each blend. Write it on the lines. Next, choose six of the blends and write another word that is not on the spelling list.**

   Spelling list: snowflake, photograph, instead, fireplace, scout, twinkle, skinny, asleep, glue, smudge, respect, pray, swiftly, control

2. Introduce vocabulary words for the story, *Matt's Birthday Blessing: The New Bike*. Use LAR page 8.

   Awesome, cafe`, enough, explanation, garage, miracle, mountain, obedient, quoted

   Have students read the vocabulary words and definitions. Next: **Read the story, Mountain Top Cafe` on the bottom of the page. Vocabulary words are missing from the story. Match the number in the blank to the words with lines at the bottom of the page. Read the story once without filling in the blanks. Read the story a second time to fill in the blanks. When you have a story with missing words, it helps to read it through once to get a better idea of what the story is about.**

3. Students will begin reading the first chapter of *Matt's Birthday Blessing: The New Bike*. Introduce the story. Have students look at the title page. Students should read the title, and the description on the title page.

   Have students find the table of contents. Have students read the chapter title for chapter 1. **What do you think this chapter is about?**

   This is a story about a boy named Matthew. He wants something new. Can you guess what it is? (A new bike) **Read Chapter 1 to see if his dad buys it for him.**

4. Use the handwriting sheet or have the children write the following sentences:

   The snowflakes twinkle in the moonlight.
   I took a photograph of the mountain.

Answers SAP page 9

gl	glue	gr	photograph
pl	fireplace	pr	pray
sc	scout	sk	skinny
sl	asleep	sm	smudge
sn	snowflake	sp	respect
st	instead	sw	swift
tr	control	tw	twinkle

Answers LAR page 8

3 awesome 1 cafe 9 enough 6 explanation 7 garage

5 miracle 2 mountain 4 obedient 8 quoted

Lesson 7

Lesson Objectives

1. Students will review nouns and verbs. (L)
2. Students will review spelling rules for suffixes. (S)
3. Students will read the story *The New Bike*. (R)
4. Students will copy sentences neatly and correctly. (H)
5. Students will write possessive nouns. (L)
6. Students will research and write about violins. (W)

Materials

LAR Workbook page 9
SAP Workbook page 10
WSW pages 6 and 7
Book: *The New Bike*
Resource Pack Rules for Forming Possessive sheet and Forming Possessives practice sheet

Teaching

1. Ask students to give simple definitions for the terms noun and verb. (Noun: person, place, or thing. Verb: things nouns do, actions) Write the sentence: **The scout found the trail**. Have students find the nouns. (scout, trail) Ask what is the verb? (found)

   LAR workbook page 9: Read the sentences. Circle the nouns. Underline the verbs. Next, choose one of the sentences and change the noun. Rewrite the new sentence. Then, choose another sentence. Change a verb and rewrite the sentence.

2. Use SAP workbook page 10. Review spelling rules for adding ing and ed. **The last consonant in short vowel words that end with a single consonant, making a single sound, is doubled before adding ing or ed. This keeps us from confusing it with long vowel words with silent e's that are dropped.**

   Example: split, splitting.

   The word doesn't need to be changed before adding ing or ed to words that end with digraphs. Example: claw, clawing **What are some other digraphs? Digraphs are two letters that represent a single sound.** (Examples include th, sh, ue, oa)

   The word doesn't need to be changed before adding ing or ed to words that end with two vowels and a single consonant. Example: feed, feeding

   The suffixes ing and ed can be added to words that end with a silent e after dropping the e. Example: spice, spicing. **Now, use the rules to add suffixes to the word list. Add i-n-g and e-d.**

3. Have students finish reading the first chapter of *The New Bike* and begin chapter two.
   Ask questions about chapter 1:

   What was Mr. Day buying at the beginning of the story? (an inner tube)
   What were some other things Matthew had really wanted in the past? (video game, Double Pump Slammers)
   Why didn't Mr. Day buy the bike? (Matthew didn't take care of his old bike.)
   What was Robert's nickname and why was it his nickname? (Rail, because he was very thin.)
   What were Matthew and Rail going to build? (a tree house)
   Why did Rail quit working on the tree house? (He had to help his mother.)

   Have students read the chapter title for chapter 2 before beginning to read.

4. Use the handwriting sheet or have the children write the following sentences:

   The people prayed for a miracle. Did the glue leave a smudge?

5. Use the Rules for Forming Possessive sheet and Forming Possessives practice sheet. Present the rules from the sheet. Next, have students write the possessive forms of nouns from the descriptions.

   The rule for proper nouns that end with s is simplified. Using an apostrophe s can also be acceptable, particularly if the added s is pronounced.

6. Students will write a story about a violin in the workbook. Before writing, students will research about violins and include some of those facts in the story. Students should include a sheet with notes from their research. References for their research should also be included. This may be the name of the book, website address, etc. The list of facts to find is a suggestion. Students do not have to find all those facts and can include other facts. As a part of the assignment, students should also find and listen to some violin music.

Rules for Forming Possessives

The possessive form of a noun shows belonging

Add an apostrophe and s to make a noun possessive.

cat: The cat's paw is fuzzy.

If a proper noun ends with s add just an apostrophe.

Thomas: Thomas' book is on the table.

To make plural nouns that end with s possessive, add just an apostrophe.

dogs: The dogs' barks were very loud.

All other nouns that end with s, add 's

bus: The bus's tire is flat.

Answers LAR page 9

The river flowed swiftly over the rocks.
The obedient child followed her father.
Ann photographed the fireplace.
The skinny kitten drank the milk.
The snowflakes melted on the driveway.

Practice Sheet Answers

The fireplace's bricks
The scout's path
Bess' glue
The snowflakes' designs
The stars' twinkling
The boss's photograph
The blueberries' taste
The creature's color

Answers SAP page 10

split splitting
claw clawing
feed feeding
spice spicing

	add ing	add ed
flake	flaking	flaked
scout	scouting	scouted
respect	respecting	respected
weed	weeding	weeded
skin	skinning	skinned
pray	praying	prayed
smudge	smudging	smudged

Lesson 8

Lesson Objectives

1. Students will identify nouns as singular or plural. (L)
2. Students will write a thank you letter. (W)
3. Students will review the beginning blends. (P)
4. Students will review spelling words. (S)
5. Students will read part of the story *The New Bike*. (R)
6. Students will copy sentences neatly and correctly. (H)
7. Stduents will write about four feelings. (W)

Materials

LAR Workbook page 10
SAP Workbook page 11
WSW page 8
Book: *Matt's Birthday Blessing: The New Bike*

Teaching

1. Write the sentences: **The big pigs ate the corn. A little pig ate oats.**

   Ask if the underlined noun in the first sentence means one or more than one animal. (More than one) **If a noun is in a form that means more than one, we say it is plural. *Pigs* is the plural form of the word *pig*. Plural means more than one.**

   Ask if the underlined noun in the second sentence means one or more than one animal. (One) **If the noun means just one, we say it is singular. The word *pig* is the singular form of the noun *pig*. Singular means just one.**

   Use the top of LAR workbook page 10: Fill in the circle that tells if the underlined noun is singular or plural.

2. Students will use the form on the bottom of LAR workbook page 10 to write a thank you letter on behalf of Matthew Day. **Matthew wants to write a thank you letter to his grandparents for the money they gave him. Use the bottom of the workbook page to help him out. The lines are color coded to guide you.**

   Most letters including thank you letters begin with a greeting. A common letter greeting is the word *Dear* spelled d-e-a-r. Write the word *Dear* on the brown lines followed by the name of the person you are writing to. Write dear with a capital letter. In this case, Matthew is writing to his grandparents. He should write something like *Dear Grandfather and Grandmother.* (Students may put in the own variation such as grandma and grandpa.)

   Next, look at the red lines. On these lines write what the people are being thanked for. *Thank you for____________.*

   Next, add what the gift meant to Matthew. Use the purple lines. You can imagine the gift was given to you, and write how it made you feel, why you are grateful, or even how you plan to use it. This is the part where you want to honor the person who gave the gift and show your appreciation. If someone was thanking you, what would make you feel good and appreciated?

   The green lines are for a closing remark, usually one or two words. For a close relative you might use the word *love. Sincerely Yours, Sincerely, Yours Truly* are common closing remarks. Can you think of others you have seen? Begin each word with a capital letter.

   Finally, the blue lines are for a signature. A signature is simply your name, or in this case, Matthew's name. It is usually written in cursive. (Students may print if they have not been taught cursive.

3. Write the letters g, p, s, t and the words lane, rip, ray, and can. **Look at the first word, *lane.* Look at the four choices of letters. Choose a letter that forms a beginning blend and a word.** (plane) Repeat with rip (trip, grip), ray (gray, tray), and can (scan)

   Use the top of SAP workbook page 11. **Add g, p, s, or t to the words to make another word.**

4. Use the bottom of SAP workbook page 11. **Find the spelling words that have the letters to make the small word on the page. You can arrange the letters in any order. The first word is *flew.* Can you find the word that has all the letters to spell *flew*?** (snowflake) **Write snowflake on the first set of lines. Complete the rest of the page.**

5. Finish reading the second chapter of *The New Bike*. Ask the students the following questions. Then begin reading chapter 3.

   What was one of Matthew's chores? (Taking out the trash)
   What was Mr. Day fixing? (Matthew's bike)
   Why do you think Matthew wanted a new bike? (Answers vary)
   Do you think he really needed a new bike? Why or why not? (Answers vary)
   Why do you think Matthew felt after talking to Rail under the tree? (Answers vary)
   Have you ever thought you really needed something, only to discover someone else had a greater need?

   Have students read the chapter title for chapter 3 before beginning to read.

6. Use the handwriting sheet or have the children write the following sentences:

   A fireplace was in the cafe. The pup fell asleep in the garage.

7. Students will write about four key words. Students should first formulate a purpose (question) for each key word. They do not have to write the question, simply have it in mind as they write. For example, using the word *comfortable,* the questions might include: What makes me feel most comfortable? How can I help a friend who is nervous feel comfortable? What makes something comfortable?

   Students should include spelling words and/or vocabulary words.

LAR Answers page 10

1. The boys are swimming in the lake.	❍ singular	● plural
2. A smudge was on the photograph.	● singular	❍ plural
3. The mountain was awesome.	● singular	❍ plural
4. We ate at the new cafe.	● singular	❍ plural
5. Two cars were in the garage.	❍ singular	● plural

SAP Answers page 11

add g p s t

s *or* t wig	g lass	s now	
s core	g *or* t rain	p lace	s wipe
g round	s park	s lime	s team
p ride	s mile	s kate	

flew	snowflake	hoot	photograph
cost	scout	sale	asleep
steer	respect	link	twinkle
yap	pray	tool	control
ate	instead	fly	swiftly
race	fireplace	gum	smudge
sink	skinny	lug	glue

Lesson 9

Lesson Objectives

1. Students will review spelling words. (S)
2. Students will read the story *The New Bike*. (R)
3. Students will learn about similes and metaphors. (L & W)
4. Students will copy sentences neatly and correctly. (H)

Materials

SAP workbook page 12
LAR workbook page 11
Book: *The New Bike*

Teaching

1. Use SAP workbook page. **Read the clues and write the spelling word that matches each clue.**
2. Ask questions about chapter 3.

   What was Matthew's surprise when he got home? ($90.00)
   Why couldn't his grandparents be with him on his birthday? (The story doesn't say. Ask students why they think the grandparents may not have waited until the next day.)
   What did Matthew mean by saying that God answered his prayer? (He had enough money to buy the bicycle.)
   Why was Rail's mother crying? (She lost her job.)
   How do you think Matthew felt? (Answers vary.)
   What do you think Matthew will do? (Answers vary.)

   Students will now read chapter 4 of the story *The New Bike*. Have students read the chapter title for chapter 4 before beginning to read.
3. Use the LAR workbook page. Have students read about similes and metaphors on the workbook page. The text is reprinted below:

   When you write a poem or a story, sometimes you can use a comparison that creates a word picture. There are two kinds of comparisons, similes and metaphors.

   A **simile** compares two things using the words *like* or *as*.

   Your smile is like a sunny day. I can run as fast as a cheetah.

   A **metaphor** compares two things and doesn't use *like* or *as*.

   The clouds were puffy balls of cotton floating in the sky.

   Students will complete the exercises on the page. **Read the three sentences. Write an S in the box before the sentence if it uses a simile. Write an M in the box if it uses a metaphor. Next, write a simile or a metaphor on the lines.**

   Have students look at the poetry they began developing in lesson 4. **Poems try to tell a story in as few words as possible. A quick and imaginative way to describe things in a poem is to use similes or metaphors. Revise your writing.** (Continued on the next page.)

Use similes or metaphors to help describe things. Look at your writing and think of ideas for possible similes or metaphors. Look at the lawn mowing example on the workbook page. The new notes are in red print. You may want to use different colors for different kinds of notes, but you don't have to. The note section is copied here:

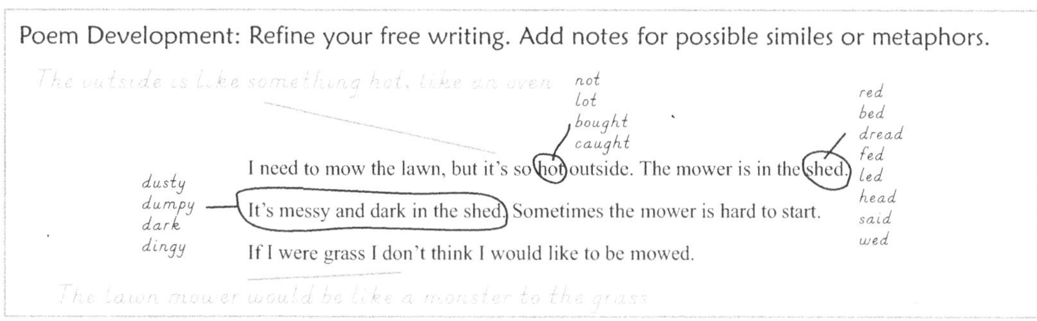

4. Use the handwriting sheet or have the children write the following sentences:

   The toy car ran by remote control.

   I will always show respect for Mom.

SAP Answers page 12

Someone who finds a path through new areas: scout	A sticky liquid: glue
To grow dim then bright over and over: twinkle	A state of thinness: skinny
A crystal of ice falling from the sky: snowflake	To talk to God: pray
A paper that has an image of something: photograph	In a state of deep rest: asleep
A box made for heating a house: fireplace	Replace with something else: instead
To show honor to someone or something: respect	Moving very quickly: swiftly
To make something do what you want it to do: control	A spot that needs cleaning: smudge

LAR Answers page 11

When you write a poem or a story, sometimes you can use a comparison that creates a word picture. There are two kinds of comparisons, similes and metaphors.

A **simile** compares two things using the words *like* or *as*.

Your smile is like a sunny day.

I can run as fast as a cheetah.

A **metaphor** compares two things and doesn't use *like* or *as*.

The clouds were puffy balls of cotton floating in the sky.

Write S or M in the boxes to identify the comparisons as similes or metaphors.

S The running children were like stampede of charging elephants.

M The apple was music to my taste buds.

S I was as frightened as a rabbit in a fox den.

Write a simile or a metaphor.

Lesson 10

Lesson Objectives

1. Students will answer questions about the story. (L)
2. Students will take a spelling test. (S)
3. Students will read a selection and make a graph. (L)
4. Students will refine creative writing. (CW)
5. Students will copy a sentence neatly and correctly. (H)

Materials

Book: *Matt's Birthday Blessing: The New Bike*
Poetry writing assignment from Lesson 9
LAR Workbook pages 12 and 13

Teaching

1. Students will read chapters 5 of *The New Bike.*
   Next, students will answer the questions about the story
   on LAR workbook page 12.

2. Have students number their paper from 1 to 14. Give the following words as dictation.

   1. glue, 2. pray, 3. snowflake, 4. scout, 5. twinkle,
   6. smudge, 7. skinny, 8. instead, 9. respect,
   10. photograph, 11. control, 12. fireplace, 13. asleep,
   14. swiftly

3. **Read the story on LAR workbook page 13 and complete the graph from the information in the story. The graph will be a bar graph. Color in the blocks to make the bar. The bars will be horizontal.**

   The story is reprinted on the next page.

4. Have students read the current versions of their poems. **Were you able to use any metaphors or similes? Were you able to use any rhymes or alliteration?**

   Give any input or ideas you may have about the poem. If students want to end a line with a rhyme and have a difficult time coming up with rhyming words, suggest moving a word or using a different word (such as a synonym) at the end of the line. There are also resources for finding rhymes such as rhyming dictionaries. A good online source is *www.rhymezone.com*. Students can find rhymes, match letters, find synonyms, antonyms, and homonyms. It is also acceptable not to follow a rhyming pattern.

5. Use the handwriting sheet or have the children write the following sentences:

   I didn't understand the explanation.
   We should always respect others.

Lesson 10

Story for Teaching part 3:

Toodles the monkey was going to have a party. It was going to be the best party ever. The party was for his good friend Gert the warthog. Toodles invited all of Gert's friends.

He knew how much they all liked to eat pies. Toodles asked all the animals he invited to tell him there favorite kind of pie. Twelve monkeys liked banana pie the best. Seven warthogs loved chocolate pie.

He asked five elephants to tell him their favorite pie. They all wanted peanut butter pie. The ten aardvarks all wanted ant pies. The nine alligators wanted monkey pie. Toodles said he would make them coconut pie instead. They said that would be fine.

With so much baking to do, Toodles decided he needed a graph. Make a graph for Toodles. Jungle animals eat a lot at parties. Each guest will get one pie. Show how many of each kind of pie Toodles will need.

Answers LAR page 12

1. B
2. A
3. A
4. C
5. C
6. B

(Sample answers for 7 & 8)

7. He cleaned it up.
8. She lost her job.
   She had to pay rent.

Answers LAR page 13

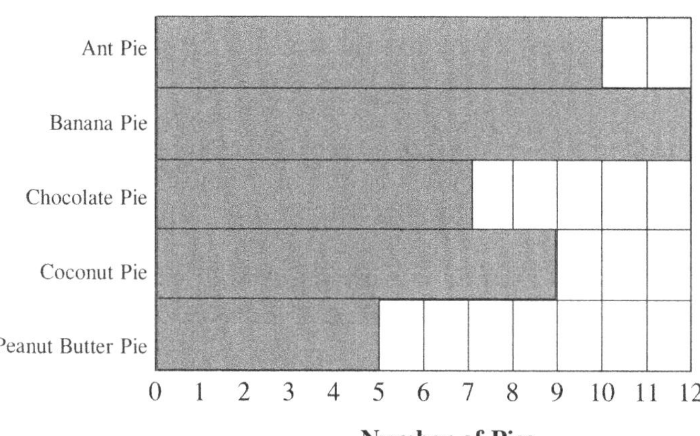

Lesson 11

Lesson Objectives

1. Students will review different spellings of the long a sound. (S & P)
2. Students will learn vocabulary words for the story *Happy Birthday, Blessing*. (L)
3. Students will review synonyms. (L)
4. Students will begin reading the story *Happy Birthday*. (R)
5. Students will copy sentences neatly and correctly. (H)

Materials

LAR Workbook page 14
SAP Workbook page 13
Book: *Matt's Birthday Blessing: Happy Birthday*

Teaching

1. Ask students if they can think of all the different ways they've learned to spell the long a sound. (a-consonant-silent e, a-consonant-y, -a-tion, -ay, -ey, -ai-, -ei-, -eig-, -eigh-, -ea-) Have students think of words that fit each of these spellings.

   Have students turn to SAP page 13. **Look at the words in the pink box. How are they all alike?** (They all have a long a sound.)
   You will do two things with the spelling list on this page. First, write the words in alphabetical order on the numbered lines. Number the words in the list first. Next, look at the sample words at the bottom of the page. Write the spelling word that spells the long a sound the same way as the sample.

2. Introduce vocabulary words for the next part of the story *Matt's Birthday Blessing*. Use the following phonetic pronunciations and definitions to introduce the vocabulary. They are at the top of LAR workbook page 12.

   envelope (en-ve-lope) *a paper folder for mailing letters*

   embarrassed (em-bare-essed) *to feel ashamed*

   disciplined (dis-i-plind) *punishment or actions taken to learn something*

   Use the top of LAR workbook page 14. **Read the sentences. A vocabulary word is missing in each sentence. Match the vocabulary words to the sentences by writing the numbers from the vocabulary list.**

3. Ask students if they know the definition of a synonym. **Synonyms are words that have similar meanings.** Ask students for examples. If students cannot think of words ask the following. **What are some synonyms for large?** (big, huge) **What are some synonyms for happy?** (glad, cheerful)

   Use the bottom of LAR workbook page 14: **Read the sentences. Substitute the words in bold print with a synonym in the word list. Fill in the circle next to the correct synonym.**

4. Have students open the book, *Matt's Birthday Blessing: Happy Birthday*, to the table of contents and read the title to chapter 1. Introduce the story.

   Have students quickly review the first part of the book. **Remember, Matthew was about to have a birthday. He wanted a bike. Let's begin reading the story to find out what he gets for his birthday present.**

   Have students now read chapter 1.

5. Use the handwriting sheet or have the children write the following sentences:

   They borrowed my toothpaste.
   The reindeer surveyed the field.

SAP Answers

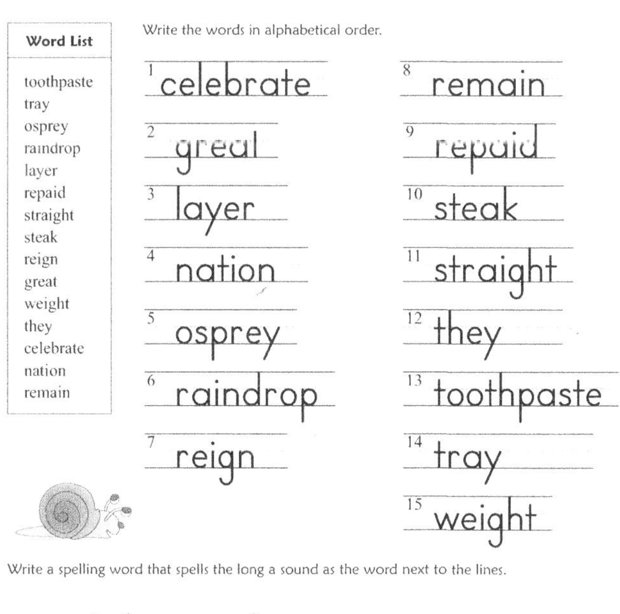

Word List
toothpaste
tray
osprey
raindrop
layer
repaid
straight
steak
reign
great
weight
they
celebrate
nation
remain

Write the words in alphabetical order.

1. celebrate
2. great
3. layer
4. nation
5. osprey
6. raindrop
7. reign
8. remain
9. repaid
10. steak
11. straight
12. they
13. toothpaste
14. tray
15. weight

Write a spelling word that spells the long a sound as the word next to the lines.

snail raindrop, remain, or repaid
survey osprey or they
break steak or great
shame toothpaste or celebrate
eight weight
jay tray or layer

LAR Answers

Read the words using the phonetic spellings and definitions.

1. **envelope** (en-ve-lope) *a paper folder for mailing letters*
2. **embarrassed** (em-bare-essed) *to feel ashamed*
3. **disciplined** (dis-i-plind) *punishment or actions taken to learn something*

2 I was ___ when everyone stared at me.

3 The pup was ___ for chewing up the shoe.

1 The letter came in a brown ___.

Read the sentences. A word is in bold print. Fill in the circle next to the word that is a synonym to the word in bold print.

1. Can you **fix** the toaster? ● repair ○ break ○ clean
2. The horse **whinnied** at me. ○ barked ● neighed ○ smiled
3. The food is on the **platter**. ○ fork ● tray ○ oven
4. The **water** fell from the sky. ○ bird ○ leaves ● raindrops
5. The sharp knife will cut the **meat**. ○ potatoes ○ paper ● steak
6. Mother told me to **remain** here. ○ leave ● stay ○ look
7. [illegible] ● [illegible]
8. I don't like feeling **ashamed**. ○ happy ○ angry ● embarrassed
9. Matthew got a **gift** for his birthday. ● present ○ cake ○ spanking
10. We must stay on the **path** in the woods. ○ sticks ● trail ○ snakes

Lesson 12

Lesson Objectives

1. Students will review pronouns. (L)
2. Students will review long a. (S & P)
3. Students will read part of *Happy Birthday.* (R)
4. Students will complete their poems. (CW)
5. Students will copy sentences neatly and correctly. (H)
6. Students will make a persuasive arguement for a toothpaste brand. (W)

Materials

LAR Workbook page 15
SAP Workbook page 14
WSW page 9
Book: *Matt's Birthday Blessing: Happy Birthday*

Teaching

1. Ask students to give simple definitions of the term pronoun. (A pronoun takes the place of a noun.) Ask students to name some pronouns. **Today we will work with the pronouns he, she, they, and it.** Read the sentence: **Dave went to the store. What pronoun can be used in place of Dave?** (He) **He went to the store.**

   Use *he* for male nouns. Use *she* for female nouns. Use *they* for plural nouns. Use *it* for singular nouns with no gender.

   Use LAR page 13: Read the sentences. Fill in the circle next to the pronouns that can take the place of the nouns in bold print.

2. Write the words *wig, red, oat.* Have students look at the spelling list on SAP page 13. **You've done spelling activities where you had to find the spelling word that used the letters from other words. Today you'll do the same thing, but you can't change the order of the letters in the small word.But,you can add other letters in between the letters. Let's look at the word *wig.* What spelling word has the letters w-i-g in that order?** (weight) Write the word *weight.* Underline the w, i, and g. Repeat with *red.* (repaid) and oat (toothpaste).

   Use the SAP workbook page. **Write the word that can be made from the small word without changing the order of the letters. Write the spelling word on the lines.**

   On the bottom part, just write in the missing letters to complete the spelling words.

3. Have students read chapter 2 of *Happy Birthday* after asking these questions about chapter 1:

   What did Matthew's dad give him? (pictures of dogs)
   What did Rachel give Matthew? (a dog dish, an old hairbrush, and a book)
   Where were they getting the dog? (from the animal shelter)
   What was Matthew's birthday cake made of? (pancakes)
   How old was Matthew on his birthday? (nine)
   Was Rachel older, or younger than Matthew? (older)

4. Students will complete poems, adding in the ideas from lessons 4, 5, and 9. The sample poem has been completed on the workbook page.

   The yard was like a blazing oven I dug into the dark and dusty shed I pulled the rope and started shovin' A roaring monster filling grass with dread

   Your poem doesn't have to be at all like the sample, but let's look at the different things that were put in the poem. The sample poem used the simile comparing the heat in the yard to a blazing oven. The second line used alliteration with the beginning letter d.

   The poem followed an ABAB rhyme pattern. The first and third lines rhymed. The second and fourth lines rhymed. The poem also uses a metaphor comparing the mower to a roaring monster. Even though the words *lawn mower* were not used in the poem, you know it was comparing the mower to a monster.

   It used something else called personification. That means pretending something has some characteristic of a person. In this case, the grass was filled with dread. What does *dread* mean? (fear) **Could grass really feel that way? Turn your notes and ideas into your own poem. Get rid of extra words and add any metaphors, similes, rhymes, and alliteration you want to use.**

5. Use the handwriting sheet or have the children write the following sentences:

   The Fourth of July is a celebration. It was the birth of our nation.

6. Students will write a commercial or ad for toothpaste. Commercials often focus on how the product will make the buyer's life better. It might make them feel better, look better, be healthier, have more fun, or be more successful. Students will name the toothpaste and draw a picture of the box it will come in. Students should give two or three reasons to buy and use it. Students should use some spelling words. The vocabulary list is more limited but encourage students to try to use at least one word.

LAR Answers

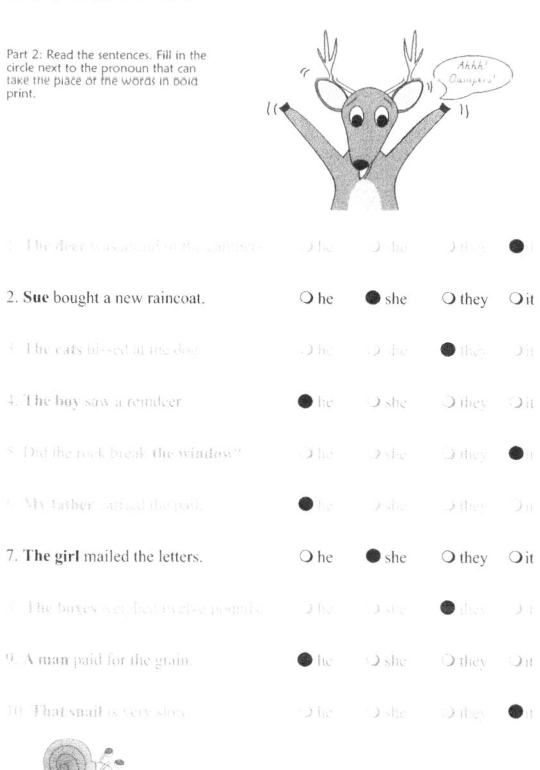

Part 2: Read the sentences. Fill in the circle next to the pronoun that can take the place of the words in bold print.

2. **Sue** bought a new raincoat. — ● she
3. **The cats** hissed at the dog. — ● they
4. **The boy** saw a reindeer. — ● he
5. Did **the rock** break the window? — ● it
7. **The girl** mailed the letters. — ● she
9. **A man** paid for the grain. — ● he
10. **That snail** is very slow. — ● it

SAP Answers

Part 1: Add letters to the words to make spelling words.

1. tea steak	2. man remain
3. and raindrop	4. rag straight
5. past toothpaste	6. read repaid
7. he they	8. ton nation
9. wet weight	10. spy osprey
11. late celebrate	12. lye layer
13. get great	14. rig reign

Fill in the missing letters in the sentences to make spelling words.

Just a little bit of toothpaste remained in the tube.

Lesson 13

Lesson Objectives

1. Students will review nouns and pronouns. (L)
2. Students will review homophones. (L)
3. Students will review the spelling list. (S)
4. Students will read part of the story *Happy Birthday*. (R)
5. Students will copy sentences neatly and correctly. (H)
6. Studtns will write about three different topics. (W)

Materials

LAR Workbook page 16
SAP Workbook page 15
WSW page 10
Book: *Matt's Birthday Blessing: Happy Birthday*

Teaching

1. Review pronouns again. Ask students to define a pronoun. (Pronouns take the place of nouns.) Review the pronouns from Lesson 12. Ask students to list them. (he, she, it, they.) Add some more pronouns: him, her, and them. Students will read the pairs of sentences on the top of LAR of workbook page 14 items 1 to 4. Students will then write the nouns that the pronouns referred to in the second sentence. For number 5 of part 1:

   Pronouns can be confusing if they are misused. Write the sentence: Ann had Beth's baseball cap. She gave it to her. Ask **who is she and who is her? It's not clear. Did Ann give it to Beth? Did Beth give it to Ann? In this case, it would have been better to just replace one of the names with pronouns, not both.**

   Have students fix the last sentence of number five by replacing one of the pronouns with a noun from the other sentence (snake or mouse). The noun and pronoun they choose changes what animal did the biting.

2. Use the bottom of LAR page 16: **Read the words. Write a homophone for each word on the lines.** (You may remind students that homophones are words that sound the same but are spelled differently.) Example: ate <u>eight</u>

3. Use SAP page 15. **You will write the spelling words by breaking a secret shape code. Look at the first row of boxes and shapes on the workbook page. This is where you will write the code. When you learn what letter a shape stands for, write the letter in the box above the shape.**

   I'll give you a few clues. First, find the longest spelling word. Fill in the boxes for the spelling word first. Next, write the letters that you solved in the key at the top. This will help you fill in letters for other words.

4. Finish reading the second chapter of *Happy Birthday*. Ask the students the following questions then begin reading chapter 3.

   What surprise did Matthew get at school? (cupcakes)
   What kind of dog did Rachel want? (a poodle)
   What did Matthew name the dog? (Buster)
   What happened when Buster saw a truck? (He chased it.)
   How did Matthew feel after yelling at Buster? (strange, hurt, sorry, but right)
   Have you ever felt that way?

5. Use the handwriting sheet or have the children write the following sentences:

   The raindrops soaked the envelope.
   A lot of weight was on the tray.

6. Three idea starters are on the page. Students will complete them. Students should try to include spelling and/or vocabulary words. You may have students write on all three topics or shorten it to one or two.

   Another alternative is to spread this activity over Lessons 14 and 15. Complete one section each lesson. For the second topic, students should understand the definition of disciplined to mean obtaining better behavior or more skills through training. For example, it takes discipline to practice and develop skill to play a musical instrument.

   Students should start writing the entire beginning sentence, not just the rest of the sentence. Students should write a paragraph with at least two supporting sentences and a concluding sentence.

LAR Answers

Break the shape code and decode spelling words.

e	w	h	g	s	b	i	t	m	d	a	r	c	o	l	n	p	y	k

they raindrop tray

straight repaid

weight nation layer

remain reign steak

great celebrate

toothpaste osprey

SAP Answers

Read the sentences. Answer the questions about the pronouns.

Stan vase

1. The cars honked at the puppy. It barked at them.
   What is them? cars What is it? puppy
2. My uncle saw my mother. He gave her a hug.
   Who is her? mother Who is he? uncle
3. Sally is nice to her brother. She gave him an ice cream cone.
   Who is him? brother Who is she? Sally
4. The crowd loved the funny monkey. They laughed at the tricks it did.
   Who are they? crowd What is it? monkey
5. The mouse saw the snake. It bit it.

Write a homophone for each word by spelling the long a sound a different way.

Example: ate eight

1. break brake
2. weigh way
3. reign rain
4. mail male
5. wait weight
6. tale tail
7. prey pray
8. grate great

US Mail

Lesson 14

Lesson Objectives

1. Students will review spelling words. (S)
2. Students will read part of the story *Happy Birthday*. (R)
3. Students will write a research report. (W)
4. Students will copy sentences neatly and correctly. (H)

Materials

SAP workbook page 16
LAR workbook page 17
Book: *Matt's Birthday Blessing: Happy Birthday*

Teaching

1. Use SAP page 16. **Match the clues to spelling words. Write the spelling words on the lines.**

2. Ask questions about chapters 3.

   Why didn't Matthew wear his boots? (He didn't want to be teased.)
   Why didn't Rachel tell on Matthew? (He would tell on her, too.)

   Students will now read chapters 4 and 5 of the story *Happy Birthday* and then ask questions.
   What happened to Matthew's boots? (Buster chewed them up.)
   What did Matthew learn from Buster? (He learned the importance of being obedient.)

   Students will now read chapters 4 and 5 of the story *Happy Birthday*.

3. The students will write a short research report from an outline with the option of using additional resources. Use LAR page 17. The steps for developing the topic from the workbook page are reprinted in bold print below. Students will not need to follow these steps to write the report about osprey, since the workbook page already does it as an example. You may have students choose a new topic and follow the steps.

   1. **Choose a topic**
   2. **Think of possible questions you or your reader might want answered. You may want to make a graphic organizer of your questions.**
   3. **Find information: websites, magazines, topical books, reference books such as encyclopedias and dictionaries, and experts. Be sure to keep track of your sources and give them credit.**

      If you copy a source word for word, be sure to use quotation marks. This indicates that you are not trying to make others think these are your own words.

      Make notes of your information. Note cards are helpful because you can rearrange them to help organize your report.

   4. **Organize your report. Make an outline or create another graphic organizer.**

   (continued on the next page)

Have students write at least a two paragraphs about osprey (or another topic). An example of turning the outline into a paragraph might look like this:

The osprey has several names. It is also known as the seahawk, fishhawk, or fishing eagle. As you can tell by its many names, the osprey lives near water. It must live near water because its favorite food is fish.

4. Use the handwriting sheet or have the children write the following sentences:

   I was embarrassed when my shirt tore.
   I repaired it with a needle and thread.

SAP Answers

toothpaste tray osprey raindrop layer repaid straight steak reign great weight they celebrate nation remain

It falls from the sky.
raindrop

Gave back what was taken
repaid

United States of America
nation

It eats fish.
osprey

Part of a stack
layer

Pounds, ounces, grams
weight

Not crooked or bent
straight

A king does it.
reign

Do this on your birthday.
celebrate

To stay behind
remain

It's better than good
great

Put this on a brush.
toothpaste

Lesson 15

Lesson Objectives

1. Students will answer questions about *Happy Birthday*. (L and R)
2. Students will take a spelling test. (S)
3. Students will put sentences from a story in the correct order. (L)
4. Students will read the reports they have written. (R)
5. Students will copy a sentence neatly and correctly. (H)
6. Students will read and respond to a fable. (R)

Materials

LAR Workbook pages 18 and 19
Resource Pack Fable Sheet

Teaching

1. Use LAR page 18. Answer the questions about the story *Happy Birthday*
2. Have students number their paper from 1 to 15. Give the following words as dictation:

   1. tray, 2. repaid, 3. reign, 4. osprey, 5. nation, 6. layer, 7. straight, 8. steak, 9. raindrop, 10. weight, 11. toothpaste, 12. celebration, 13. great, 14. remain, 15. they
3. Students will read the story on LAR page 19 and number each set of sentences in the correct order from 1 to 4. The text from the page is printed below:

   Dark clouds rolled over the forest. Soon, large raindrops began to fall. The animals ran for shelter. The army of ants scrambled for their hole in the ground. That is, all except one. Elma the ant was tugging a strange object. She had found it at a campsite. It had the letters t-o-o-t-h-p-a-s-t-e printed on it.

   "Plug the hole!" yelled the commander of the ant troop. His name was Bizmo. "The water must remain outside."

   "But Elma is not here. We can't leave her outside," said another ant.

   Water was already beginning to fill the hole. Bizmo surveyed the rushing water. "We must think of what is best for all," said Bizmo. "We have to stop the water. The whole ant nation is at risk."

   The ants tried to plug the hole. The weight of the water was too great. Elma tugged and tugged when she saw what was happening. Suddenly a great gush of water picked up the tube of toothpaste. Elma hopped on.

   It floated right to the ant's hole. Elma jumped into the hole. Then a tree limb crashed down. It landed on the tube. Toothpaste squirted into the hole. The water stopped running in. Elma's toothpaste had stopped the water. The ants were saved.

   The next day was clear and sunny. The ants had a celebration for Elma. They wanted to repay her for being so brave. Then they had a great feast. The ants thought the toothpaste tasted very yummy.

4. Have students read the research reports written in lesson 14.
5. Use the handwriting sheet or have the children write the following sentences:

   The girl had wavy hair.
   The lost dog remained in the neighborhood.

6. Use the Fable Sheet. Students will read the fable *The Tortoise and the Ducks*. Students will explain what the fable means in their own words.

LAR Answers page 18

1. A
2. B
3. C
4. C
5. B
6. A

Answers can vary for 7 & 8

7. For disobeying by wearing lipstick.
8. It doesn't feel good to have to discipline someone. Discipline teaches us to obey. It's for our own good.

LAR Answers page 19

Set 1	Set 3
2	3
1	2
3	1

Set 2	Set 4
2	1
3	3
1	2

Lesson 16

Lesson Objectives

1. Students will review different spellings of the long i sound. (P)
2. Students will spell words correctly. (S)
3. Students will learn vocabulary words for the story *The Wrong Goal.* (L)
4. Students will begin reading the story *The Wrong Goal.* (R)
5. Students will copy sentences neatly and correctly. (H)
6. Students will write an imaginary interview. (W)

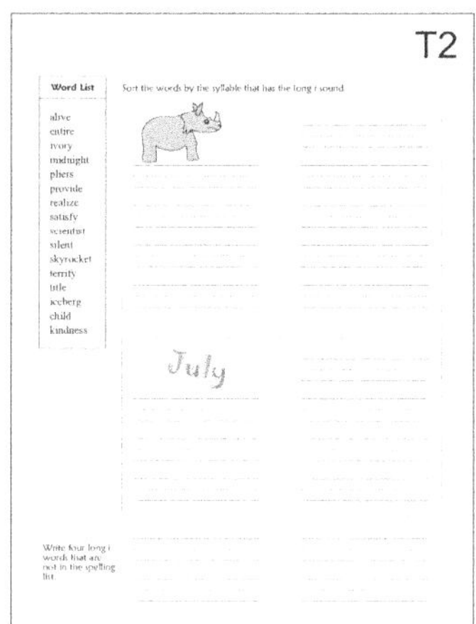

Materials

SAP Workbook page 17
LAR Workbook page 20
WSW page 11
Book: *The Wrong Goal*

Teaching

1. Ask students if they can think of all the different ways they've learned to spell the long i sound. (i-consonant-e, ie, igh, uy, y, -ild, -ind) Have students think of words that fit each of these spellings.

   Point out the rule for words ending in y. Write the words funny and my. **Can you tell me why the y sound changes?** (More than one syllable, y has the long e sound. One syllable, y has the long i sound.) **There is an exception to this rule found in the spelling list: satisfy. The letters –fy are a suffix. The y has the long i sound. Other words have this suffix such as *electrify, terrify, defy,* and *edify.***

2. Spelling List: alive, entire, ivory, midnight, pliers, provide, realize, satisfy, scientist, silent, skyrocket, terrify, title, iceberg, child, kindness.

   Review syllables. Write the words *behind, sign,* and *recognize.* **Read the first word. How many syllables does it have?** (2) **Be-hind. Remember each syllable has a vowel sound. You can also clap on the syllables to help count them.** Demonstrate by saying and clapping once on each syllable of *behind.* Have students count syllables for *sign* and *recognize.*

   Use the SAP workbook page. **Read the words. What vowel sound do they all have in common?** (Long i) **Most of the words have more than one syllable. Sort and write the words by the syllable that has the long i sound. If the long i sound is in the first syllable like the word *rhinoceros* or only syllable, write the word in the top box. If the long i is in the last syllable, like the word *July*, write the word in the second box. Write four more long i words that are not in the spelling list.**

3. Introduce vocabulary for the story *The Wrong Goal.* Have students look at the title page. Students should read the title and the description on the title page. Introduce the vocabulary words:

   laboratory, explosion, customer, occasionally, millionaire,
   invention, ordinary, identification, artificial

   Use LAR page 20. **Read the definitions of the words. Use the words in the sentences. Write the words on the lines.**

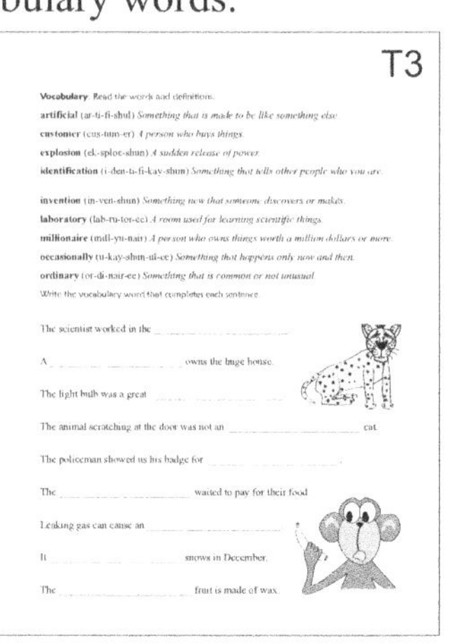

4. Introduce the story. **This is a story about a girl named Allison Jones. Allison is a ten-year-old girl who likes to help her father in his scientific laboratory. What do you think it would be like to work in a laboratory? What kinds of discoveries or inventions would you like to make?**

   Students will begin reading the first chapter of *The Wrong Goal.*

5. Use the handwriting sheet or have the children write the following sentences:

   The scientist worked in the laboratory.
   Did the skyrocket explode?

6. The students should pretend they are millionaires being interviewed for a magazine. Write answers to the questions the reporter is asking them. One the bottom section, students will make up one more question they would ask a millionaire. Students should try to use spelling and vocabulary words.

LAR Answers

Vocabulary: Read the words and definitions.

artificial (ar-ti-fi-shul) *Something that is made to be like something else.*

customer (cus-tum-er) *A person who buys things.*

explosion (ek-sploe-shun) *A sudden release of power.*

identification (i-den-ti-fi-kay-shun) *Something that tells other people who you are.*

invention (in-ven-shun) *Something new that someone discovers or makes.*

laboratory (lab-ru-tor-ee) *A room used for learning scientific things.*

millionaire (mill-yu-nair) *A person who owns things worth a million dollars or more.*

occasionally (u-kay-shun-ul-ee) *Something that happens only now and then.*

ordinary (or-di-nair-ee) *Something that is common or not unusual.*

Write the vocabulary word that completes each sentence.

The scientist worked in the laboratory.

A millionaire owns the huge house.

The light bulb was a great invention.

The animal scratching at the door was not an ordinary cat.

The policeman showed us his badge for identification.

The customer waited to pay for her food.

Leaking gas can cause an explosion.

It occasionally snows in November.

The artificial fruit is made of wax.

SAP Answers

Top box 1st syllable long i	Bottom Box Last syllable long i
ivory	alive
pliers	entire
scientist	midnight
silent	provide
skyrocket	realize
title	satisfy
iceberg	terrify
child	
kindness	

Lesson 17

Lesson Objectives

1. Students will review long i. (S & P)
2. Students will add suffixes to words. (S)
3. Students will review adjectives. (L)
4. Students will read the story *The Wrong Goal*. (R)
5. Students will copy sentences neatly and correctly. (H)
6. Students will describe the parts and function of a tool. (W)

Materials

SAP Workbook page 18
LAR Workbook page 21
WSW page 12 and a pair of pliers, nuts and bolts if available
Book: *The Wrong Goal*

Teaching

1. Use the SAP workbook page. Students will write the spelling words that have the letters to make the smaller words.
2. Review adding ing and ed to words. Review rules:
    1. Silent e's are dropped: hope, hoping, hoped
    2. The last consonant of a short vowel syllable is doubled unless it is part of a consonant blend: begin, beginning, ship, shipped. This rule does not apply to x (box, boxing, boxed) because it represents two sounds, ks, but the word *skyrocket* in this lesson is an exception to the rule. The t does not double.
    3. Drop the y and add ied: hurry, hurried. Don't drop the y when adding ing (hurry, hurrying) because -ing is a new syllable.
    4. Just add the suffix to words with vowel digraphs or consonant blends (oil, oiled, oiling, hint, hinted, hinting).

    Use the bottom of the SAP page. **Add ed and ing to the spelling words. Don't forget to apply the spelling rules.**
3. **What does an adjective do**? (An adjective helps describe a noun.) Introduce the term modify. **An adjective modifies a noun. Name some adjectives.** (pretty, happy, big, little, etc.)

    Listen to this sentence. Find the adjective: The loud duck quacked at night. What is the adjective? (loud) **Listen to this sentence and add an adjective. The cat is purring.** (example answers: fuzzy, brown, big)

    Use LAR page 21: Read the sentences. Fill in the circle next to the word that is used as an adjective in the sentence.
4. Have students finish reading the first chapter of *The Wrong Goal* and begin chapter two. Ask these questions about chapter 1:

    What two things did Allison smell at the mailbox? (honeysuckle and smoke)

    What word did people use to describe Winston Jones? (puzzling)

    (continued on the next page)

Where had Allison and her mother been? (at the grocery store)

What caught on fire? (grass)

What was Onyx? (a computer)

5. Use the handwriting sheet or have the children write the following sentences:

   Elephant tusks are made of ivory.

   Her diary is supposed to be private.

6. If possible provide a pair of pliers for students to explore and perhaps nuts and bolts. Students will write about pliers. You may have students do research on the tool, but students can also derive information just by examining and using a pair of pliers. Three parts of pliers are labeled. Students will describe the use and/or physical description of each part. Students will then write about how pliers can be used.

LAR Answers

1. five
2. new
3. quiet
4. blue
5. hot
6. apple
7. rare
8. mild
9. nice
10. red

SAP Answers

Find the spelling word that has the letters to make the small word.

teen	entire
roy	ivory
lid	child
thin	midnight
send	kindness
fire	terrify
nest	silent
slip	pliers
test	scientist
tilt	title
veal	alive
rice	iceberg

Add ing and ed to the spelling words. Use the spelling rules.

	Add ed	Add ing
provide	provided	providing
realize	realized	realizing
satisfy	satisfied	satisfying
skyrocket	skyrocketed	skyrocketing

Lesson 18

Lesson Objectives

1. Students will compare present and past tense verbs. (L)
2. Students will review the spelling list. (S)
3. Students will change vowel sounds in words. (P & S)
4. Students will read part of the story *The Wrong Goal*. (R)
5. Students will copy sentences neatly and correctly. (H)

Materials

LAR Workbook page 22
SAP Workbook page 19
Book: *The Wrong Goal*

Teaching

1. Write the sentences: We ran to the tree. We are running to the tree. **How are the sentences are alike?** (They're both about running to a tree.) **How are they different?** Underline the words ran and running. Introduce the concept of tense. **Verbs have tense. The tense of a verb tells when it happened. *Ran* is the past tense. *Are running* is the present tense.**

   The word *are* helps determine the tense. It is a helping verb. The words *is*, *am*, and *are* tell present tense. The words *was* and *were* tell past tense.

   LAR page 22: **Read the sentences. Underline the verb. Fill in the circle that tells whether the sentence happened in the past or present. Next, read the two sentences with lines. Change the tense of the verbs and rewrite the sentences.**

2. Have students categorize the spelling words by how the long i sound is spelled. Use SAP page 19 to sort the words.

3. Write the words *rip, sped,* and *kid.* **What letters can you add to the words to make the vowel sound a long i? Look at the first word. It has the short i sound. Read the word.** (rip) **Now replace the vowel sound with long i and say it again.** (ripe) **What letter will you add to the word *rip* to make it *ripe?*** (e) Repeat with sped (spied). The word *kid* is a little different because it needs an n to make the word *kind.*

   Use the bottom section of SAP page 19. **Add letters to words to make them have the long i sound.**

4. Finish reading the second chapter of *The Wrong Goal*. Ask the students the following questions then begin reading chapter 3.

   How would you describe the FRV-7? (a saucer-shaped object that flies)
   What did Megan do wrong? (She kicked the ball into the wrong goal.)
   What did Allison say to the other girls about Megan? (She wanted Megan to quit the team.)
   What did Winston feel about challenges? (He liked them.)
   How would you help solve Allison's problem? (Answers vary.)

5. Use the handwriting sheet or have the children write the following sentences:

   The explosion happened at midnight.
   The invention replaces pliers.

LAR Answers

1. driving present
2. flying present
3. liked past
4. stopped past
5. walked past

The scientist made a new invention.
The customer is buying the artificial flowers.

SAP Answers

1. alive, ivory, entire, provide, realize, silent, iceberg, title
2. child, kindness
3. midnight
4. pliers, scientist
5. satisfy, skyrocket, terrify

1. time	2. dried
3. guy	4. quite (or quiet)
5. fried	6. fight
7. eye	8. fire

Lesson 19

Lesson Objectives

1. Students will review spelling words. (S)
2. Students will read the story *The Wrong Goal*. (R)
3. Students will describe an invention. (CW)
4. Students will copy sentences neatly and correctly. (H)
5. Students will write possessive nouns. (L)

Materials

SAP Workbook page 20
LAR Workbook page 23
Book: *The Wrong Goal*
Resource Pack Rules for Forming Possessive sheet and Forming Possessives practice sheet

Teaching

1. Use the SAP page. **Write the spelling word that matches each clue.**

2. Ask questions about chapter 3.

   How did Allison think her invention would help Megan? (It would make her a soccer superstar.)
   What did Allison give Megan? (a headband)
   Why did Megan kick the ball at the bird's nest? (The bird had the flower.)
   What carried the flower to the popcorn stand? (a chipmunk)
   Did Allison mean to get Megan in trouble? (no) **How do you know this?** (Answers vary. She wanted to make Megan a superstar. Allison wasn't the one who moved the flower.)
   Why did Megan think Allison meant to get her into trouble? (She had heard that Allison wanted her off the team.)

   Students will now read chapter four of the book *The Wrong Goal*.

3. Have the students think of an invention. Students will write about it by answering the questions on LAR page 23. Extra space is on the page to make a drawing of the invention.

4. Use the handwriting sheet or have the children write the following sentences:

   Did you recognize the millionaire?
   The customer did not have identification.

5. Use the Rules for Forming Possessive sheet and Forming Possessives practice sheet. Present the rules from the sheet. Next, have students write the possessive forms of nouns from the descriptions.

   The rule for proper nouns that end with s is simplified. Using an apostrophe s can also be acceptable, particularly if the added s is pronounced.

Rules for Forming Possessives

The possessive form of a noun shows belonging

Add an apostrophe and s to make a noun possessive.

cat: The cat's paw is fuzzy.

If a proper noun ends with s add just an apostrophe.

Thomas: Thomas' book is on the table.

To make plural nouns that end with s possessive, add just an apostrophe.

dogs: The dogs' barks were very loud.

All other nouns that end with s, add 's

bus: The bus's tire is flat.

Practice Sheet Answers

The iceberg's size
The bass's weight
Mrs. Lukens' kindness
The skyrocket's glow
The scientists' plan
The steak's smell
The tray's weight
Ross's pliers

SAP Answers

Use the clues to find the spelling words. A list is in the orange box.

alive entire ivory midnight pliers provide realize satisfy scientist silent skyrocket terrify title iceberg child kindness

It goes up very fast.
skyrocket

midnight

It's very cold
iceberg

A tool
pliers

Being nice
kindness

Quiet
silence

Give what is needed
provide

Not dead
alive

Make very afraid
terrify

Elephant tusk
ivory

satisfy

title

Lesson 20

Lesson Objectives

1. Students will answer questions about the story *The Wrong Goal.* (L)
2. Students will take a spelling test. (S)
3. Students will follow directions. (L)
4. Students will read the stories they have written. (R)
5. Students will copy a sentence neatly and correctly. (H)
6. Students will read and respond to a fable. (R)

Materials

Creative writing assignment
LAR Workbook pages 24 and 25
Crayon
Resource Pack Fable Sheet

Teaching

1. Use LAR workbook page 24. Answer the questions about the story.

2. Have students number their paper from 1 to 16. Give the following words as dictation.

   1. silent, 2. ivory, 3. pliers, 4. satisfy, 5. kindness, 6. entire, 7. iceberg, 8. title, 9. scientist, 10. alive, 11. child, 12. provide, 13. realize, 14. midnight, 15. terrify, 16. skyrocket

3. It's important to follow directions. Students will read the directions to mark the pictures at the bottom of the page on workbook page 25.

   Winston needed to take the FRV-7 for some test flights. Allison made a map of the farm. It was her job to give her father directions. After each flight the FRV-7 flew back to the launch pad and started over.

   Read the directions and write where the FRV-7 went on each test flight.

4. Have students read stories from the lesson 19 creative writing assignment.

5. Use the handwriting sheet or have the children write the following sentences:

   The entire crowd was silent.
   Do you like that style of buildings?

6. Use the Fable Sheet. Students will read the fable *The Dog, the Rooster, and the Fox*. Students will retell the order of events using words that show order such as first, second, next, last.

LAR Answers page 24

1. A
2. C
3. C
4. B
5. B
6. B
7. C
8. C

9 & 10 Answers vary. Sample answers:

9. She was a star. She played very well.
10. She learned to care about Megan.
    She learned helping people was more important than soccer.

LAR Answers page 25

1. field
2. flower garden
3. bird's nest
4. house
5. pond
6. flock of geese
7. laboratory
8. barn

Lesson 21

Lesson Objectives

1. Students will review different spellings of the long o sound. (S & P)
2. Students will learn vocabulary words. (L)
3. Students will begin reading the story *One Is Enough* part 1. (R)
4. Students will copy sentences neatly and correctly. (H)

Materials

SAP Workbook page 21
LAR Workbook page 26
Book: *One Is Enough* part 1

Teaching

1. Ask students if they can think of all the different ways they've learned to spell the long o sound. (o-consonant-e, consonant-o, ow, oa, ough, oe) Have students think of words that fit each of these spellings.

   Use the SAP page. **Look at the words in the pink box. Find words that match each long o spelling pattern: o-consonant-e, consonant-o, o-w, o-a, ough, o-e. Spell the words out loud.** Have students look at each word and decide which pattern each word fits.

   Next, write the words in alphabetical order. At the bottom of the page, think of three more long o words and write them on the lines. Use words with different spelling patterns.

2. Use LAR page 26. **Read the definitions of the vocabulary words for the story *One Is Enough* part 1. Next read the story with missing words twice. Read it once without filling in the blanks. Next, read it and fill in the blanks with vocabulary words. Write the number from the blank next on the lines next to the vocabulary word at the bottom of the page.**

   List: companies, cousin, curiosity, different, disappointed, electricity, machine

3. Students will begin reading the first chapter of *One Is Enough* part 1. Introduce the story. Have students look at the title page. Students should read the title and the description on the title page.

   This is another story about Allison Jones. This is only the first half of the story. The next book contains the second part. If students have used the First or Second grade McRuffy curriculum, ask them about Emily and Elaine Rose. **What do they remember about them?** (They are identical twins. Elaine causes a lot of problems. Emily doesn't.) **In this story, we learn that Allison Jones is their cousin.**

4. Use the handwriting sheet or have the children write the following sentences:

   We had a snowstorm at Christmas.
   Do you know the location of the hotel?

Lesson 21

LAR Answers

Read the story. Match the blanks to vocabulary words. Write the numbers next to the words at the bottom of the page.

My __1__ Karen said she was taking me to a show. I expected to see a movie or play. Then she told me it was a __2__ kind of show.

When businesses want people to see the things they make, they have shows. Lots of __3__ had their products on display.

There were many unusual inventions. One __4__ created lots of __5__. I had never seen anything like it. It looked like it was holding two pizzas.

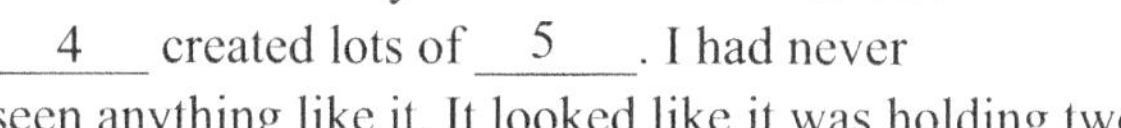

NASA's Phoenix Mars Lander

A lady told me that the discs were covered with solar cells. The solar cells let the machine make __6__ from sunlight. The machine was being made to explore the planet Mars. I really enjoyed the show. Although it wasn't a movie, I wasn't __7__.

3 companies 1 cousin 5 curiosity 2 different

7 disappointed 6 electricity 4 machine

o-consonant-e
explode

consonant-o
tornado echo
gross hotel
location automobile
avocado

o-w
snowstorm
overflow
wheelbarrow

o-a
raincoat
toaster

ough
doughnut

o-e
poem
toenails

SAP Answers

Write the words in alphabetical order.

Word List
tornado
snowstorm
explode
gross
location
overflow
avocado
poem
echo
doughnut
hotel
raincoat
automobile
toaster
toenails
wheelbarrow

1 automobile
2 avcocado
3 doughnut
4 echo
5 explode
6 gross
7 hotel
8 tornado
9 location
10 overflow
11 poem
12 raincoat
13 snowstorm
14 toaster
15 toenails
16 wheelbarrow

Write three other long o words that are not on the spelling list.

Lesson 22

Lesson Objectives

1. Students will write spelling words. (S)
2. Students will review long o words.
3. Students will use irregular nouns. (L)
4. Students will read the story *One Is Enough* part 1. (R)
5. Students will copy sentences neatly and correctly. (H)
6. Students will compare characters in two different stories. (W)

Materials

SAP Workbook page 22
LAR Workbook page 27
WSW page 13
Book: *One Is Enough* part 1

Teaching

1. Use the top of SAP page 22. **Write the spelling words that have the letters to make the short words.**

2. Use the bottom of SAP page 22: **Add the missing letters in the words to make long o words. Write the words on the lines.**

3. Ask students to give simple definitions for the term noun. (A noun is a person, place, or thing.) Write the words dog and puppy. Introduce irregular plural nouns: **We change nouns from the singular to plural forms by adding s or changing the ending and adding s. If you have more than one dog, you just add s (dogs). Sometimes you have to drop a y and add ies. Look at the word *puppy*. Let's make it plural. The spelling changes a little** (write puppies)**, but the root word is still *puppy*. Irregular nouns are words that don't form plurals in the normal way. An example of an irregular noun is foot. What word do you use to mean more than one foot?** (feet) **It's not *foots*. It's *feet*. The word changed. Some irregular nouns change into different words to mean one or more than one. Some irregular nouns don't change at all to mean one or more than one. For example, *sheep* can mean one sheep or many sheep.**

   Write the words shelf and knife. **Nouns that end with the f sound change in a different way when they are made plural. We say one shelf and two shelves. What happened to the f sound in shelves?** (It changed to the v sound.) **To make these words plural, change f to v and add es to the end of the word. How do you write the plural of *knife*?** (knives)

   LAR page 27. **Write the word that means more than one of each noun. Next, complete the sentences by writing the singular or plural form of the noun. You may use a dictionary.**

4. Have students finish reading the first chapter of *One Is Enough* part 1 and begin chapter two. Ask questions about chapter 1:

   How did the angry looking man hurt Allison's feelings? (He told her to leave.)
   What did Winston say the man wanted him to play? (God)
   What did Winston mean by that? (The man wanted him to do something that only God should do.)
   Why didn't Allison eavesdrop using her computer? (Onyx told her it was wrong.)
   What was Allison's idea for the science fair? (She didn't have one yet.)

5. Use the handwriting sheet or have the children write the following sentences:

   Did the invention explode?
   A gross is twelve dozen.

6. Students will compare the characters from the last two stories. Students may refer to reading books as a resource. Students will answer the questions to make the comparisons.

LAR Answers

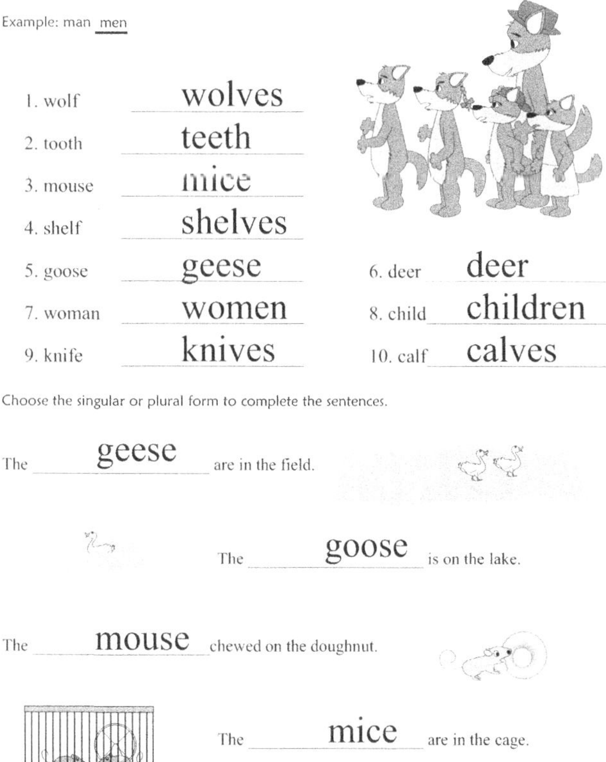

SAP Answers

Add letters to the words to make the long o sound. Rewrite the words on the lines.

Example: flat float

1. hop	hope	2. g	go
3. cat	coat	4. to	toe
5. tough	though	6. he	hoe
7. cost	coast	8. n	no
9. gal	goal	10. glob	globe

Lesson 23

Lesson Objectives

1. Students will identify different kinds of sentences (questions or statements). (L)
2. Students will review the spelling list. (S)
3. Students will make new words. (P)
4. Students will read part of the story *One Is Enough* part 1. (R)
5 Students will copy sentences neatly and correctly. (H)
6. Students will write facts and opinions (W)

Materials

LAR Workbook page 28
SAP Workbook page 23
WSW pages 14 and 15
Book: *One Is Enough* part 1

Teaching

1. Introduction: **There are different kinds of words in sentences such as nouns, verbs, adjectives. There are also different kinds of sentences. Two kinds of sentences are statements and questions. What do you think the difference between a statement and a questions is?** (A statement tells something. A question asks something.) **What do we write at the end of a sentence that is a question?** (a question mark) **What do you think we write at the end of a statement?** (period)

   LAR page 26: **Read the sentences. Fill in the box at the beginning of the sentence with a Q if it is a question. Write S if the sentence is a statement. Put the correct ending mark (question mark or period) at the end of the sentence.**

   Next, write one statement and one question.

2. Use the top of SAP page 23. **Fill in the vowels to make spelling words.**

3. Write the words bobcat, firecracker, and buttercup. **Read the first word.** Add words to the list: place, wild, fly, sun. **If I took off the first part of *bobcat,* what word do I have?** (cat-erase or mark out *bob*) **I'll add a new beginning to the word.** (add *wild* to the beginning to make the word *wildcat).* **Read the new word.**

   What word from my second list can I use to make a new word out of *firecracker?* (place) **What's the new word?** (fireplace) **What new word can I make from buttercup?** (butterfly)

   Use the bottom of SAP page 23. **Replace parts of the spelling words to spell other words. Choose new parts from the box.**

4. Finish reading the second chapter of *One Is Enough* part 1. Ask the students the following questions then begin reading chapter 3.

   Why do you think this chapter is called Two Roses For Allison? (Emily and Elaine's last name is Rose.)
   What did Emily and Elaine talk about on the way to Allison's house? (Funny stories about what each sister had done.)
   What is the name of Allison's mother? (Anna)
   What did all the green and red lights in the laboratory remind Emily of? (Christmas)
   Why did Elaine go into Winston's office? (She heard a noise.)
   What did she see on Winston's desk? (a top secret envelope)
   What do you think the secret project was? (Answers vary.)

5. Use the handwriting sheet or have the children write the following sentences:

   The toaster needs electricity.

   Is my raincoat in the wheelbarrow?

6. This lesson has two pages. The first page develops the concepts of facts and opinions. Have students read the examples at the top of the page. Discuss the difference with the students. **Read the three facts. We know that cats have whiskers, because we can look at them and see whiskers. We can look at a thermometer and find the temperature. A person's name can be proven with all kinds of records such as a birth certificate.**

   Look at the opinions. Some people are allergic to cats. A cat wouldn't make a good pet for them. Perfect isn't a measurement of temperature. Some people might wish it were warmer or cooler. Maybe there are people who don't feel that Joe is nice.

   Students will mark the answers for the bottom of the sheet. The facts are items 1, 4, 7, 8, and 10. The opinions are items 2, 3, 5, 6, and 9.

   Students will write a fact and an opinion represented by each picture on the second page. Students can do additional research if necessary but shouldn't need to. Students should include spelling and/or vocabulary words. The pictures are of an avocado, doughnut, and an antique automobile.

LAR Answers

Part 1: Read the sentences. Write a Q in the box if the sentence is a question. Write an S if the sentences a statement. Put the correct ending marks at the end of the sentences, periods or question marks.

Q 1. Do Inuit people make igloos___

S 2. The electricity went off at the hotel___

S 3. My poem was very different___

Q 4. Where is the old automobile___

Q 5. Did the sink overflow___

Q 6. How did my raincoat get ripped___

S 7. My cousin loves avocados___

Q 8. Who unplugged the toaster___

S 9. The wheelbarrow lost a wheel___

Q 10. Why do doughnuts have holes___

Part 2: Write a statement and a question.

Statement:

Question:

SAP Answers

Fill in the vowels to make spelling words.

overflow location avocado

tornado explode gross snowstorm

toenail automobile toaster

wheelbarrow doughnut echo

poem hotel raincoat

Trade parts of the spelling words to make new words. Use a part from the word list.

Word list
thunder
matic
fill
pea
finger
cart
bow

snowstorm thunderstorm

overflow overfill

doughnut peanut

automobile automatic

wheelbarrow cartwheel

toenail fingernail

raincoat rainbow

Lesson 24

Lesson Objectives

1. Students will review spelling words. (S)
2. Students will read the story *One Is Enough* part 1. (R)
3. Students will write a paragraph. (W)
4. Students will copy sentences neatly and correctly. (H)

Materials

SAP Workbook page 24
LAR Workbook page 29
Book: *One Is Enough* part 1

Teaching

1. Use SAP page 24. **Write the spelling words that match the clues.**
2. Ask questions about chapter 3.

   What was Allison's problem at the beginning of the chapter? (She needed to make her science project, but she wanted to play with her cousins.)
   Who thought of an idea for Allison's science project? (Elaine)
   How were the girls going to make the machine work? (It didn't really have to work.)
   How did they make it look like it worked? (They added Christmas lights and recorded a humming sound.)
   What did the machine pretend to do? (make copies of people)
   Who did Allison choose to make a copy of? (Emily)
   What was she going to make the copy from? (Fluffy the dog)

   Students will now read chapter four of the book *One Is Enough* part 1.

3. Use the LAR page. Students will read about constructing a paragraph and see an example for the creative writing assignment. The LAR page is reprinted on the next page. The bottom of the page includes lines to help organize a paragraph. The sample paragraph is color coded for the various parts. The topic sentence is purple. The supporting sentences are red. The closing sentence is green.

   In chapter 2, Emily and Elaine told Allison funny stories that had happened to each other. Write about something funny that's happened to you, your brother or sister, or even a friend. Write at least one paragraph. Look at the workbook page and read about making a good paragraph. You can make notes on the bottom of the page for your story. Write your story on another piece of paper.

   The first word in a paragraph is indented. This means it's moved to the right. This helps the reader see where a new paragraph begins when you write more than one paragraph.

4. Use the handwriting sheet or have the children write the following sentences:

   I ate a doughnut and an avocado.
   Our cousin hurt his toenail.

Lesson 24

Writing a good paragraph

A paragraph has three parts. It begins with a **topic sentence**. It has **supporting sentences** that add details. It ends with a **closing sentence** that sums up the paragraph's main idea. Include all three parts for a well constructed paragraph.

A funny thing happened *Angie burnt a doughnut*

Detail 1 *Angie watched Mom put a bagel in the toaster.*

Detail 2 *Angie wanted a warm doughnut.*

Detail 3 *The toaster started smoking.*

indent the first word in a paragraph →

My little sister, Angie, learns the funniest things from watching others. One day she got a doughnut stuck in the toaster. She had watched mom heat up a bagel. Angie thought it was a doughnut. She wanted a warm doughnut, too. When the toaster started smoking, Angie thought it was going to explode. She ran screaming to my mother. Mom didn't think it was too funny when she saw the mess, but I couldn't stop laughing.

Make notes to write a paragraph about a funny event.

A funny thing happened ______________________________

Detail 1 ______________________________

Detail 2 ______________________________

Detail 3 ______________________________

SAP Answers

Drive it.

automobile

It can heat food

toaster

[illegible]

tornado

[illegible]

poem

Where it is

location

Boom!

explode

Twelve dozen

gross

They're at the end of a foot.

toenails

Can't be filled any fuller

overflow

It only has one tire.

wheelbarrow

A place to stay

hotel

It's when sound bounces back.

echo

[illegible]

avocado

It keeps you dry.

raincoat

Lesson 25

Lesson Objectives

1. Students will answer questions about the story *One Is Enough* part 1. (L)
2. Students will take a spelling test. (S)
3. Students will recall details. (L)
4. Students will read the stories they have written. (R)
5. Students will copy a sentence neatly and correctly. (H)
6. Students will read and respond to a fable. (R)

Materials

Creative writing assignment
LAR Workbook page 30
Resource Pack Fable Sheet

Teaching

1. Use the top of LAR page 30. Answer the questions about the story.

2. Have students number their paper from 1 to 16. Give the following words as dictation.

   1. avocado, 2. doughnut, 3. overflow, 4. raincoat, 5. automobile, 6. toenails, 7. explode, 8. echo, 9. gross, 10. toaster, 11. tornado, 12. wheelbarrow, 13. location, 14. poem, 15. snowstorm, 16. hotel

3. Use the bottom of LAR workbook page 25. Students will read the paragraph. Students will then answer the questions.

4. Have students read stories from the lesson 24 creative writing assignment.

5. Use the handwriting sheet or have the children write the following sentences:

   The poem is about a tornado.
   The automobile was a great invention.

6. Use the Fable Sheet. Students will read the fable *Belling the Cat.* Students will then write a short fable with the same moral or lesson. Students will write about something that is easy to suggest, but hard to do.

LAR Answers

Part 1

1. B. Elaine
2. C. People Copy Machine
3. B. Fluffy
4. A. Anna
5. C. She needed a science fair project.

Part 2

1. wagons
2. self
3. able to be moved

Lesson 26

Lesson Objectives

1. Students will read and spell oo words correctly. (S)
2. Students will review homophones. (L)
3. Students will learn vocabulary words. (L)
4. Students will begin reading the story *One Is Enough* part 2. (R)
5. Students will copy sentences neatly and correctly. (H)

Materials

LAR Workbook pages 31
SAP Workbook page 25
Book: *One Is Enough* part 2

Teaching

1. Ask students if they can think of words spelled with oo. There are four different sounds. The oo sound in moon is commonly called the long oo sound. The oo sound in book is commonly called the short oo sound. In the words blood and flood the oo makes a short u sound. In the words door and poor oo makes the o + r sound.

   SAP page 25: **Sort the spelling words by the sounds the o-o makes. Match the words to the pictures: moose, football, duck, and horse. The word with two oo sounds has its own space with two pictures.**

2. **Homophones are words that sound alike, but have different spellings and meanings. For example the words *too, two,* and *to*.** Ask students if they can think of examples.

   Use the top of LAR page 31. **Read the letter. It is full of homophones, but the wrong words were used. These words are in color print. Write the correct words on the lines.**

3. Introduce the vocabulary words for the story. Use the bottom of LAR page 31. **Read the words and definitions. Write the vocabulary words that complete the sentences.**

   Attention (a-ten-shun) *To listen or watch closely*

   Recognize (re-cog-nize) *To know what something is or know who someone is*

   Underneath (un-der-neeth) *below something*

   Warehouse (ware-hous) *A large building used to store things*

4. Students will begin reading the first chapter of *One Is Enough* part 2. It is numbered chapter five since it is a continuation of last week's story. Have students briefly review what happened in the first part of the story.

   Read chapter 5 in *One is Enough* Part 2.

5. Use the handwriting sheet or have the children write the following sentences:

   The bloodhound howled at the poodle.
   The cartoon was about a kangaroo.

LAR Answers

Read the letter. The words are wrong. The words in color print are the homophones for the correct words. Write the correct words on the lines under the letter.

Deer Sally,

I've been meaning to right you for sum time. I can't weight to [illegible] you again. You don't no how I've missed ewe. Wood you visit me soon?

Eye maid a cake this [illegible]. It didn't cost much. The flower was on sail. I eight most of it. It tasted grate. I'll bake you [illegible] when you come.

Your Friend,

Buzz.

Dear write some wait see
know would made morning
flour ate great one

Vocabulary words for *One is Enough* part 2.

Attention (a-ten-shun) *To listen or watch closely*
Recognized (re-cog-nized) *To know what something is or know who someone is*
Underneath (un-der-neeth) *below something*
Warehouse (ware-hous) *A large building used to store things*

The warehouse was full of boxes.

I did not recognize you in that costume.

You should pay attention to your parents.

There is a badger underneath the porch.

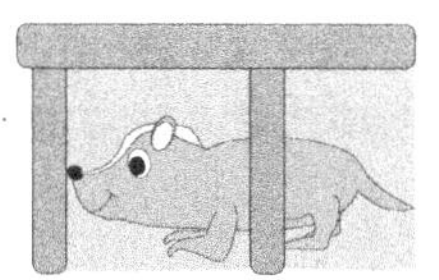

SAP Answers

Word List
understood
bookmark
footstool
mongoose
cartoon
bloodhound
mood
bamboo
doorknob
flood
goodnight
kangaroo
moonlight
poodle
school
woodpecker

Sort the words by the vowel sound that oo makes. Match the sounds to the pictures: moose, football, duck, and horse.

mongoose
cartoon mood
bamboo kangaroo
moonlight poodle
school

footstool

woodpecker understood
bookmark goodnight

bloodhound flood

doorknob

Lesson 27

Lesson Objectives

1. Students will review parts of speech. (P)
2. Students will identify helping verbs. (L)
3. Students will review spelling words. (L & S)
4. Students will read the story *One Is Enough* part 2. (R)
5. Students will copy sentences neatly and correctly. (H)
6. Students will research and write facts. (W)

Materials

LAR Workbook page 32
SAP Workbook page 26
WSW page 16
Book: *One Is Enough* part 2

Teaching

1. Review parts of speech: noun, pronoun, verb, adverb, and adjective. **What is a noun?** (person, place, or thing) **What is a verb?** (It is a word that tells what a noun is doing.) **What is a pronoun?** (a word that takes the place of a noun.) **What are some examples of pronouns?** (she, he, her, they, we, it)

   What is an adverb? (It is a word that describes a verb.) **Many adverbs end with the suffix l-y, like quickly and softly. What is an adjective?** (It is a word that describes a noun.) **Some adjectives include tall, short, soft. Adjectives include colors and numbers such as seven red flowers.** Use the top of the LAR page. **Read the sentences. Parts of the sentences are in different colors. Fill in the circle that shows what each part of speech the color word is. Mark your answer on the matching color row.**

2. To introduce the concept of a helping verb write the following sentences. Pete ran to the school. Pete is running to the school. Pete is a bunny.

   Ask students to find the verb in the first sentence. (ran) Ask students to find the verb in the second sentence. The word running is a verb. Have students read the third sentence. **What is the verb?** (is)

   Look at the second sentence again. Is the word *is* in this sentence also? (yes) **The second sentence has two verbs together, *is* and *running*. *Running* is the main verb.** Have students read the sentence without the word is (Peter running to the school.) **It just doesn't sound right.**

   The verb *running* needs help. That's why the word *is* was added. It helps out the main verb. In the second sentence, the word is is a helping verb.

   Other helping verbs include: am, are, was, and were. These normally come before the main verb.

   Part 2 of LAR page 32: **Read the sentences. Circle the helping verb. Underline the verb it helps.**

3. Use SAP page 26. **Do you remember what analogies are? Analogies compare two sets of words. The two words in the first set are alike in some way and the second set of words are alike in the same way.**

   Look at the first set of analogies and complete it with a spelling word. *Day is to Monday as goose is to*____. What spelling word completes the analogy? (mongoose) **Both *day* and *goose* have the letters m-o-n added to the beginning. In the bottom section, unscramble the spelling words.**

4. Have students finish reading the first chapter (Chapter 5) of *One Is Enough* part 2 and begin chapter six. Ask questions about chapter 5:

   Where did Elaine say she got the idea for the People Copy Machine? (From Winston's office)
   Did Allison's parents know where she was? (no)
   What were the men going to do before unloading the boxes? (Eat pizza or find a good place for them.)
   Why did a buzzer sound? (It was the pizza delivery person.)
   What did Allison see when she was looking for Elaine? (Elaine's hand reaching for pizza)

5. Use the handwriting sheet or have the children write the following sentences:

   Did the flood reach the school?
   The flute was made of bamboo.

6. Students will write five facts about kangaroos and woodpeckers. Students may research to find facts. Students should try to include spelling and/or vocabulary words. It may not be possible to use very many.

LAR Answers

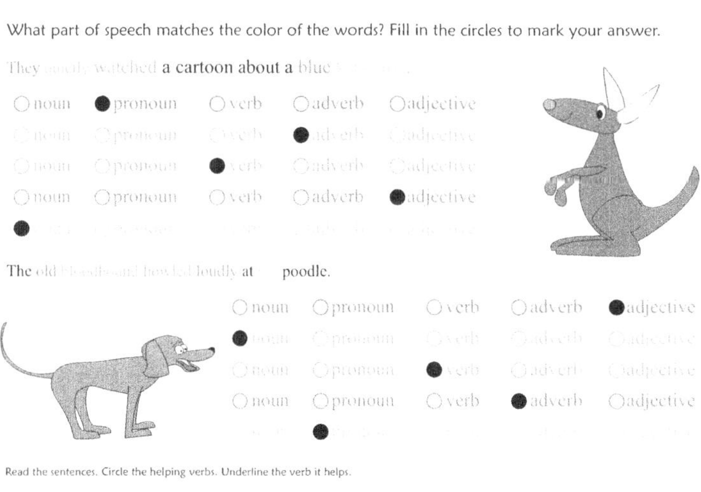

1. The mongoose (was) <u>chasing</u> the snake.
2. The poodles (were) <u>barking</u> at the cats.
3. The slippers (are) <u>falling</u> off the footstool.
4. A cartoon (is) <u>playing</u> on the television.
5. I (am) <u>working</u> at the warehouse.
6. The woodpecker (was) <u>hunting</u> for bugs.
7. The children (were) <u>leaving</u> the school.
8. The kangaroo (is) <u>hopping</u> across the yard.
9. I (am) <u>paying</u> attention to my mother.
10. The bloodhounds (are) <u>howling</u> in the moonlight.

SAP Answers

Lesson 28

Lesson Objectives

1. Students will unscramble sentences. (L)
2. Students will combine sentences. (L)
3. Students will review the spelling list. (S)
4. Students will read part of the story *One Is Enough* part 2. (R)
5. Students will copy sentences neatly and correctly. (H)
6. Students will write opinions. (W)

Materials

LAR Workbook page 33
SAP Workbook page 27
WSW page 17
Book: *One Is Enough* part 2

Teaching

1. **Use the top of LAR workbook page 33. Unscramble and write the sentences.**
2. Use the bottom of the LAR page. **Sometimes short sentences can be combined.** Write the sentences: All kangaroos have long tails. Only female kangaroos have pouches. **I can take words out if I combine sentences.**

   Often we use the words *but* or *and* to combine sentences. Use *and* if you are adding details. Use *but* to point out a difference. Write the sentence: All kangaroos have long tails, but only females have pouches. **This combines the two sentences. What word did I leave out?** (kangaroos) **What word did I add?** (but) **I also needed a comma before *but*. This means you pause briefly when reading. It shows a change in the sentence.**

   Write the sentences: My poodle has curly hair. My poodle has short legs. **I can rewrite these sentences using the word and.** Write: My poodle has curly hair and short legs. **What words were left out?** (My poodle has)

   Look at the sentences at the bottom of the workbook page. Combine the sentences. Use *and* in the first sentence. Use *but* in the second sentence.
3. Use SAP page 27 top section: **Break the code to write spelling words.**

   Begin with the shortest word. Fill in the letter code at the top of the page as you find letters and fill in the boxes to write spelling words.

   On the bottom section, write spelling words to complete the sentences.
4. Finish reading chapter 6 of *One Is Enough* part 2. Ask the students the following questions, then begin reading chapter 7.

   Who were the men going to kidnap? (the president)

   What was the man planning on doing with the president? (make himself look like the president.)

   What did Elaine act like when she got caught? (a dog)

   Why was it quick thinking to act like a dog? (The men wouldn't ask Elaine why she was there.)

   Where did Elaine go? (out the window)

   How did Allison trick the man who caught her? (She tricked him into trying to make a copy of himself. She locked him in the box.)

5. Use the handwriting sheet or have the children write the following sentences:

   I said goodnight to the mongoose.
   A woodpecker is in the garage.

6. Students will write opinions about school. Students should try to include spelling and/or vocabulary words. Questions are on the page.

LAR Answers

The moose was chewing the leaves.
We baked the cookies in the oven

(Other answers are possible for combining sentences.)
Woodpeckers have long and sticky tongues.
Bamboo is very light, but strong.

SAP Answers

Break the shape code and decode spelling words.

d	m	c	o	f	e	n	t	b	l	r	a	s	g	u	h	p

mood mongoose poodle

understood school

bloodhound bamboo

cartoon footstool

Fill in spelling words to complete the sentences.

1. A _______________ lives in the tree. woodpecker
2. The overflowing river began to _______________ the fields. flood
3. I told dad _______________ before going to bed. goodnight
4. The _______________ had a long tail and a pouch. kangaroo
5. I placed the _______________ after the page I was reading. bookmark
6. The _______________ turned, then the door opened. doorknob
7. The _______________ made it easier to see at night. moonlight

Lesson 29

Lesson Objectives

1. Students will make inferences to answer questions. (L)
2. Students will review spelling words. (S)
3. Students will read the story *One Is Enough* part 2. (R)
4. Students will write a story. (CW)
5. Students will copy sentences neatly and correctly. (H)

Materials

LAR workbook page 34
SAP workbook page 28
Book: *One Is Enough* part 2

Teaching

1. **Sometimes when we read something, not everything is told to us. You can tell what the writer is probably talking about without all the information being written. For example: Spot barked as he chased the cat up a tree. What is Spot? Spot is probably a dog. The sentence doesn't say Spot was a dog.**

   When we decided that Spot was a dog, we made an inference. An inference is a very good guess based on the things we do know. We know dogs bark. We know they chase cats. We also know that Spot did those things, so we can infer that Spot is a dog.

   LAR Workbook page 34: Read the sentences. Make inferences to answer the questions.

2. Use the clues to write spelling words on the SAP workbook page.

3. Ask questions about chapter 7.

   What did Elaine land on after jumping out a window?
   (a mattress in a truck)
   How did the woman know where to take Fluffy?
   (She looked at his dog tag.)
   How did Elaine fly the FRV-7?
   (She didn't. Onyx did by remote control. Elaine told him where to go.)
   What are some of the things the FRV-7 can do?
   (float, fly, let you talk to Onyx)
   Why do you think Onyx made the saucer fly off the cliff?
   (Answers vary.)
   What do you think will happen to Elaine and the FRV-7?
   (Answers vary.)

   Students will now read chapter eight of the book *One Is Enough* part 2.

4. **You have now built the all new FRV-8. It can do even more than the FRV-7. Where would you go? What would people do when they saw you? What special things can the FRV-8 do? Write a story about your adventure in the FRV-8.**

5. Use the handwriting sheet or have the children write the following sentences:

   The warehouse was full of footstools.
   I recognized the bookmark.

Lesson 29

LAR Answers

Wording may vary, but generally should be:

1. The baseball broke it.
2. It was raining.
3. They burned in the oven.
4. It spilled on the floor.
5. A tooth was getting loose.

SAP Answers

Use the clues to find the spelling words. A list is in the orange box.

understood bookmark footstool mongoose cartoon
bloodhound mood bamboo doorknob flood goodnight
kangaroo moonlight poodle school woodpecker

Prop your feet up on it.

footstool

mood

Too much water

flood

I knew what it meant.

understood

A place to learn

school

Give it a turn to get in.

doorknob

It is a funny drawing.

cartoon

A strong, light stalk.

bamboo

It shines in the darkness.

moonlight

It lives in Australia.

kangaroo

It's not a bird, but its name sounds like it is.

mongoose

It drills holes in trees.

woodpecker

Say it right before bedtime.

goodnight

bookmark

A dog with short, straight hair

bloodhound

A dog with curly hair

poodle

Lesson 30

Lesson Objectives

1. Students will answer questions about the story *One Is Enough* part 2. (L)
2. Students will take a spelling test. (S)
3. Students will read the stories they have written. (R)
4. Students will copy a sentence neatly and correctly. (H)
5. Students will write addresses in sentences. (L)

Materials

Creative writing assignment
LAR Workbook page 35
Resource Pack: Rules for Commas in Addresses sheet and Writing Addresses in Sentences Practice Sheet

Teaching

1. Use LAR page 35. **Answer the questions on the workbook page about the story *One is Enough*. Use complete sentences. You may use your book to find the answers.**

2. Have students number their paper from 1 to 16. Give the following words as dictation:

   1. understood, 2. flood, 3. kangaroo, 4. footstool, 5. bookmark, 6. moonlight, 7. cartoon, 8. woodpecker, 9. bamboo, 10. school, 11. bloodhound, 12. poodle, 13. doorknob, 14. goodnight, 15. mongoose, 16. mood

3. Have students read stories from the lesson 29 creative writing assignment.

4. Use the handwriting sheet or have the children write the following sentences:

   The dog was in a very bad mood.
   Nobody understood why.

5. Use the Rules for Commas in Addresses sheet to present using commas in addresses:

   When writing an address on an envelopethe only comma needed is between the city and the state for US addresses. Then use the Writing Addresses in Sentences Practice Sheet. If students don't know addresses for the practice sheet, they can make them up.

   If students need additional practice after this lesson, students can repeat with the same practice sheet and make up new addresses or write sentences about other addresses on blank paper.

Rules for Commas in Addresses

When writing an address on an envelope the only comma needed is between the city and the state for US addresses.

Ruff McRuffy
123 Woof Rd
Pupville, MO 64003

When writing an address in a sentence, use commas between the street address, city, and state or country. If a zip code is used, the two letter state abbreviation is used for addresses in the United States.

Ruff lives at 123 Woof Road, Pupville, MO 64003.

Ruff was born at 456 Barker Lane, Growler, Missouri.

His grandfather once visited London, England**.**

Ruff's mother grew up in Rover, California**.**

LAR Answers

(Key parts of answers. Wording may vary.)

1. **What does the FRV in FRV-7 stand for?** (It stands for Fire Rescue Vehicle)
2. **The man that was kidnapped was the president of what?** (bank or First Underwood Bank)
3. **Elaine and Onyx solved a problem that Winston had with the FRV-7. What was that problem?** (It was hard to fly.)
4. **What did the police think when they first saw the FRV-7?** (They thought they were being invaded from outer space.)
5. **Why do you think the story was called One Is Enough?** (People don't need copies of themselves. One is enough. Other answers can be acceptable.)

Lesson 31

Lesson Objectives

1. Students will review different spellings of the long e sound. (P)
2. Students will review antonyms. (L)
3. Students will spell sixteen words correctly. (S)
4. Students will begin reading the story *Like Layers of an Onion.* (R)
5. Students will copy sentences neatly and correctly. (H)

Materials

LAR Workbook page 36
SAP Workbook page 29
Book: My Shoes Got the Blues story 1, *Like Layers of an Onion*

Teaching

1. Ask students if they can think of all the different ways they've learned to spell the long e sound. (consonant-e, ee, ey, ea, ie, y) Have students think of words that fit each of these spellings.

   Point out the rule for words ending in y. Write the words funny and my. Ask students if they can tell why the y sound changes. (More than one syllable, y has the long e sound. One syllable, y has the long i sound.)

   Use the top of the LAR page. **Read the descriptions. Write a long e word that matches the description.** You may want give the students the word list: thief, feet, me, monkey, beach, happy.

2. Ask students if they know the definition of an antonym. ***Antonym* is another word for opposite.** Ask students for examples. If students cannot think of words ask the following. **What are some antonyms for large?** (tiny, small, little) **What are some antonyms for happy?** (sad, angry)

   Use the bottom of the LAR page: **Read the sentences. Substitute the words in bold print with an antonym in the word list. Fill in the circle next to the antonym.**

3. Use the SAP page. **This week's spelling list features words with the long e sound. Read the words in the list. Alphabetize the list. Write three more long e words at the bottom of the page.**

4. Students will begin reading the first chapter in the book, *My Shoes Got the Blues*. Chapters one to four are a story named, *Like Layers of an Onion.* Introduce the story. Have students open the book to the contents page. Have students read the chapter titles for the first four chapters. Ask the children what they think this story is about.

   Tell students that this is a story about Matthew and Buster. Have students quickly review the last story. **Remember, Matthew received a puppy for his birthday. Taking care of a pet means taking responsibility for it. Matthew finds this out in this story.**

5. Use the handwriting sheet or have the children write the following sentences:

Sally's teacher gave a speech.
Forty families listened to her.

LAR Answers

Part 1

1. me
2. monkey
3. thief
4. happy
5. beach
6. feet

Part 2

1. deep
2. He
3. mean
4. brief
5. grumpy
6. clean
7. weep
8. real

SAP Answers

Word List

between
speech
weekend
teaspoon
disappear
teacher
reason
piece
shield
turkey
money
family
forty
grumpy
everything
fourteen

Write the words in alphabetical order.

1. between
2. disappear
3. everything
4. family
5. forty
6. fourteen
7. grumpy
8. money
9. piece
10. reason
11. shield
12. speech
13. teacher
14. teaspoon
15. turkey
16. weekend

Write three other long e words that are not on the spelling list.

Lesson 32

Lesson Objectives

1. Students will review long e. (P)
2. Students will review adverbs. (L)
3. Students will review spelling words. (S)
4. Students will read the story *Like Layers of an Onion.* (R)
5. Students will copy sentences neatly and correctly. (H)
6. Students will research and write about turkeys. (W)

Materials

LAR Workbook page 37
SAP Workbook page 30
WSW page 18
Book: *My Shoes Got the Blues*

Teaching

1. Part 1 of LAR workbook page 37: Add the missing letters in the words to make long e words. Write the words on the lines.

2. Ask students to give simple definitions for the term *adverb.* (An adverb helps describe a verb.) An adverb modifies a verb. Ask students to name some adverbs. (slowly, fast, sadly, etc.)

   Part 2 of LAR workbook page 37: Read the sentences. Fill in the circle next to the word that is an adverb in the sentence. Bonus question for number 10: **What is the other adverb used in the sentence?** (easily)

3. Use the SAP workbook page. **Write the spelling word that has all the letters used in the small word.**

4. Have students finish reading the first chapter of *Like Layers of an Onion* and begin chapter two. Ask questions about chapter 1:

   Who owned the vegetable garden? (Mr. Johnson)
   How did people feel about Mr. Johnson? (No one talked to him. They thought he was an angry person.)
   What did Matthew climb when he heard Mr. Johnson? (an apple tree)
   What did Matthew throw at the bulldog? (a bucket of blue paint)

5. Use the handwriting sheet or have the children write the following sentences:

   A piece of turkey was on the tray.
   The money seemed to disappear.

6. Students should research to find at least three facts about wild turkeys. Students will then write a short story about turkeys. It should include the facts from their list. It should also include spelling words. There are no vocabulary words this week.

   Ideas for the story might include a walk in the woods and encountering a turkey. It could be a story about a wild turkey coming into their house. It could be a story about a turkey and a predator or other animal. It can be realistic or fanciful.

LAR Answers

Part 1

1. forty	2. chief
3. beast	4. weed
5. silly	6. feast
7. meet (or meat)	8. turkey

Part 2

1. quickly
2. softly
3. briefly
4. deeply
5. slowly
6. badly
7. swiftly
8. loudly
9. fiercely
10. cheaply

SAP Answers

Find the spelling word that has the letters to make the small word.

ice	piece	sheep	speech
spare	disappear	men	money
open	teaspoon	sore	reason
toy	forty	dish	shield
here	teacher	need	weekend
mug	grumpy	green	everything
true	turkey	fly	family
web	between	torn	fourteen

Lesson 33

Lesson Objectives

1. Students will use adverbs in sentences. (L)
2. Students will complete sentences using spelling words. (S & L)
3. Students will review the spelling list. (S)
4. Students will read part of the story *Like Layers of an Onion*. (R)
5. Students will copy sentences neatly and correctly. (H)
6. Students will compare pairs of words. (W)

Materials

LAR Workbook page 38
SAP Workbook page 31
WSW page 19
Book: *My Shoes Got the Blues*

Teaching

1. Review adverbs again. Ask students to define an adverb. (Adverbs modify verbs.)

   LAR workbook page 38: Read the sentences. Write the sentences again using an adverb.

2. Use the top of SAP page 31. **Complete the sentences using spelling words. A word list is in the box.**
3. Have students categorize the spelling words by how the long e sound is spelled: ee, ea, ie, y, ey.

   Use the bottom of SAP workbook page 31 to list the words.

4. Finish reading the second chapter of *Like Layers of an Onion*. Ask the students the following questions then begin reading chapter 3.

   What did Matthew break in the garden shed? (a window)

   What did Matthew do to the garbage can? (He bent the lid.)

   How did Matthew break the shovel? (It got stuck. The handle broke when he pulled it down.)

   How did Matthew fix the fence? (He glued it.)

   What would you have done? (Answers vary.)

   What did Buster do with the glue bottle? (He played with it.)

   What happened to the bird? (It landed in the glue.)

5. Use the handwriting sheet or have the children write the following sentences:

   The hedge shielded out the sunshine.

   Steve was grumpy all weekend.

6. Choose 3 word pairs. Write about how the words in those pairs are alike and/or different.

LAR Answers

Answers vary.

SAP Answers

Fill in the missing spelling words in the sentences. Use the words in the list.

weekend disappear teacher turkey family grumpy

Did the turkey disappear at Thanksgiving?

My family went to the beach for the weekend. other answers may be possible

The teacher was in a grumpy mood.

Categorize the spelling words by they way the long e sound is spelled.

1. The letters ee between, speech, weekend, fourteen

2. The letters ie piece, shield

3. The letters ey turkey, money

4. The letters ea teaspoon, disappear, teacher, reason

family, forty, grumpy, everything

Lesson 34

Lesson Objectives

1. Students will review spelling words. (S & L)
2. Students will read the story *Like Layers of an Onion.* (R)
3. Students will learn about cause and effect. (L)
4. Students will write a story. (CW)
5. Students will copy sentences neatly and correctly. (H)

Materials

LAR page 39
SAP page 32
Book: *My Shoes Got the Blues*

Teaching

1. Use SAP workbook page 32. **Write the spelling word that matches each clue.**

2. Ask questions about chapter 3.

   What was stuck to the fence? (a sparrow)
   What happened to Buster's fur? (Things stuck to it because of the glue.)
   How did Matthew's parents hear about the bright, blue bulldog? (from one of the animal control worker's radio)
   Why was the worker going to call the police? (He thought a gang had torn things up.)
   What did Mr. Johnson do when he heard the truth? (He laughed.)
   Do you think Mr. Johnson was as bad as people said? (Answers vary.)
   Why? (Answers vary.)

   Students will now read chapter four of the book *Like Layers of an Onion.*

3. Review cause and effect. State a cause: **It began to rain.** Have students think of an effect, such as: The people opened their umbrellas.

   Use LAR workbook page 39 Students will match the causes to the effects. Then students will write a sentence stating a cause and a sentence telling the effect.

4. The students will write a story starting with a single idea or fact. Givethe following introduction.

   In the story *Like Layers of an Onion*, **one bad thing led to another. This is called cause and effect. For example, Matthew put a ladder up to the fence.** (the cause) **The fence board broke.** (the effect)

   Write a story about a series of causes and their effects. Story starters might be: "I left my bicycle in the driveway." or "The latch on the hamster's cage broke."

5. Use the handwriting sheet or have the children write the following sentences:

   There are fourteen teaspoons on the table.
   Everything was ready for the party.

Lesson 34

LAR Answers

1. C
2. E
3. G
4. D
5. A
6. I
7. H
8. B
9. F

SAP Answers

Use the clues to find the spelling words. A list is in the orange box.

between speech weekend teaspoon disappear
teacher reason piece shield turkey money
family forty grumpy everything fourteen

Parents and children

family

[illegible]

teacher

A part of

piece

A big bird

turkey

Using a voice

speech

After thirteen

fourteen

A piece of silverware

teaspoon

A bad mood

grumpy

Opposite of nothing

everything

Why

reason

In the middle

between

Twenty plus twenty

forty

Can't see it anymore

disappear

[illegible]

weekend

A sheet of metal

shield

It's easy to spend.

money

Lesson 35

Lesson Objectives

1. Students will answer questions about the story *Like Layers of an Onion*. (L)
2. Students will take a spelling test. (S)
3. Students will read the stories they have written. (R)
4. Students will copy a sentence neatly and correctly. (H)
5. Students will write possessive nouns. (L)

Materials

Creative writing assignment
LAR Workbook pages 40
Resource Pack Rules for Forming Possessive sheet and Forming Possessives practice sheet

Teaching

1. Use LAR workbook page 40. Answer the questions about the story.

2. Have students number their paper from 1 to 16. Give the following words as dictation.

   1. fourteen, 2. teacher, 3. everything, 4. forty, 5. reason, 6. teaspoon, 7. shield, 8. money, 9. speech, 10. between, 11. piece, 12. weekend, 13. turkey, 14. disappear, 15. family, 16. grumpy

3. Have students read stories from the lesson 34 creative writing assignment.

4. Use the handwriting sheet or have the children write the following sentences:

   What was the reason he gave you?
   Did she feed the reindeer?

5. Use the Rules for Forming Possessive sheet and Forming Possessives practice sheet. Present the rules from the sheet. Next, have students write the possessive forms of nouns from the descriptions.

   The rule for proper nouns that end with s is simplified. Using an apostrophe s can also be acceptable, particularly if the added s is pronounced.

Rules for Forming Possessives

The possessive form of a noun shows belonging

Add an apostrophe and s to make a noun possessive.

cat: The cat's paw is fuzzy.

If a proper noun ends with s add just an apostrophe.

Thomas: Thomas' book is on the table.

To make plural nouns that end with s possessive, add just an apostrophe.

dogs: The dogs' barks were very loud.

All other nouns that end with s, add 's

bus: The bus's tire is flat.

Practice Sheet Answers

The kangaroo's bouncing
The poodle's name
Mr. Jones' poem
The turkey's feathers
The avcados' ripeness
Last weekend's storm
Chris' favorite cartoon
The lens's size

LAR Answers

Part 1

1. C
2. A
3. A 4. B
5. C 6. A
7. C 8. B

Lies have many layers, like onions.

Lesson 36

Students will use Lessons 36 to 38 to prepare for the first test. Concepts will be reviewed. A reading book is not assigned for this week. The test will be given during Lessons 39 and 40. Students will be tested over language concepts, vocabulary development, reading comprehension, and spelling.

Lesson Objectives

1. Students will review vocabulary words. (L)
2. Students will review parts of speech. (L)
3. Students will spell words correctly. (S)
4. Students will copy sentences neatly and correctly. (H)

Materials

LAR Workbook page 41
SAP Workbook page 33

Teaching

1. The following words were chosen from the vocabulary lists for each book.

   consequences, eavesdrop, cafe, obedient, embarrassed, envelope, laboratory, invention, artificial, curiosity, disappointed, attention, recognized, cousin

   Have students copy the list. Use part 1 of LAR page 41. Have students match the descriptions using vocabulary words.

2. Review the terms *noun, verb, pronoun, adverb, adjective,* and *helping verb*. Have students say definitions and examples of each.

   Use part 2 of LAR workbook page 41. Read the sentences. Students will find the word in the sentences that fit each part of speech.

3. Use SAP page 33. **Alphabetize the review spelling words on the top part. Switch parts of words on the bottom part to correct the spelling words.**

4. Use the handwriting sheet or have the children write the following sentences:

   I bought a doughnut at the cafe`.
   The automobile belongs to my cousin.

LAR Answers

Part 1

1. cafe`
2. envelope
3. laboratory
4. artificial
5. cousin
6. disappointed and embarrassed
7. eavesdrop

Part 2

1. noun	poodle	pronoun	He	adjective	injured
verb	carrying	adverb	carefully	helping verb	was
2. noun	nets	pronoun	They	adjective	slippery
verb	tugging	adverb	fiercely	helping verb	were
3. noun	automobile	pronoun	us	adjective	blue
verb	honking	adverb	loudly	helping verb	is

SAP Answers

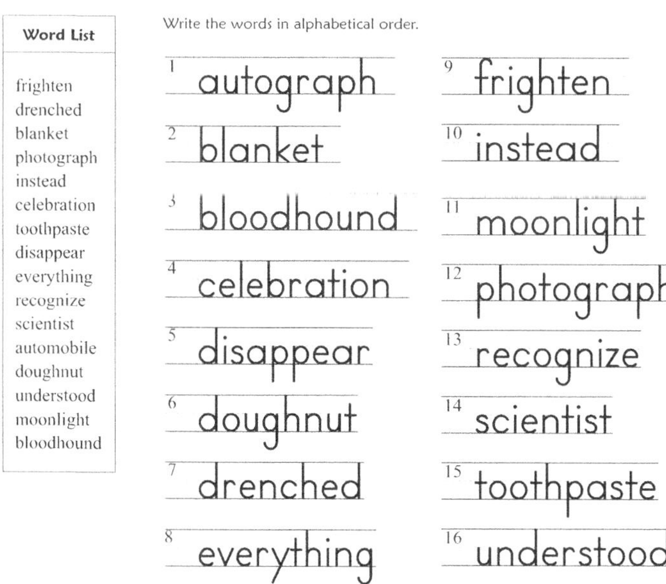

Word List

frighten
drenched
blanket
photograph
instead
celebration
toothpaste
disappear
everything
recognize
scientist
automobile
doughnut
understood
moonlight
bloodhound

Write the words in alphabetical order.

1. autograph
2. blanket
3. bloodhound
4. celebration
5. disappear
6. doughnut
7. drenched
8. everything
9. frighten
10. instead
11. moonlight
12. photograph
13. recognize
14. scientist
15. toothpaste
16. understood

Parts of words are mixed up on each switch.
Switch the letters and write the spelling words.

Answers can be switched from top to bottom

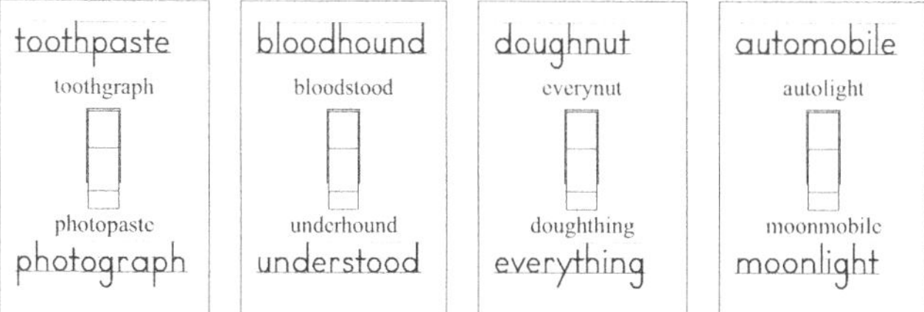

toothpaste	bloodhound	doughnut	automobile
toothgraph	bloodstood	everynut	autolight
photopaste	underhound	doughthing	moonmobile
photograph	understood	everything	moonlight

Lesson 37

Lesson Objectives

1. Students will review vocabulary words. (L)
2. Students will review tense (present and past). (L)
3. Students will review comprehension skills. (R)
4. Students will review spelling words. (S)
5. Students will copy sentences neatly and correctly. (H)
6. Students will complete similes. (W)

Materials

LAR Workbook page 42
SAP Workbook page 34
WSW page 20

Teaching

1. Have students write sentences using vocabulary words.
2. Review present and past tense. Use the top of LAR page 42. Read the sentences. Underline the verb. Is the underlined verb present or past tense? Fill in the correct circle.
3. Read the paragraph on the bottom of LAR workbook page 42. Answer the questions.
4. Use the top of SAP page 34. **Find the spelling word that has the letters needed to spell the short word.**
5. Use the handwriting sheet or have the children write the following sentences:

   The scientist worked in the laboratory.

   A photograph was in the envelope.
6. Complete the similes. A simile has two parts. The first part is the real object or subject. The second part is a comparison to that real object. The top section gives the first parts of similes. Students will write the second part. The bottom section gives the second part. Students write the first part. You may have students write responses for each simile part or let them pick 3 of each.

   Help students brainstorm a response as an example.

   What would you expect a scientist visiting your classroom to be like? (maybe serious, silly, entertaining, clumsy, boring, entertaining.) Develop the response. For example: silly.
   What else is silly? (maybe a clown in a circus.) The scientist who came toour classroom is as silly as a clown in a circus.

   Brainstorm for part 2. **How would wrapping up in a wet blanket feel?** (cold, miserable, uncomfortable) For example miserable. **What would be a misreable circumstance, probably something that didn't involve being wet, because that is what we're comparing it to.** For example: sitting alone on the bench. Sitting alone on the bench was like wrapping up in a wet blanket.

LAR Answers

Part 1

1. past
2. present
3. present
4. past
5. present

Part 2

1. brown or gray
2. snakes and birds
3. 16 to 24 inches
4. bears
5. Joey
6. Tuesday

SAP Answers

Find the spelling word that has the letters to make the small word.

lamb	automobile	deer	drenched
troop	photograph	dipper	disappear
blond	bloodhound	thud	doughnut
energy	everything	gift	frighten
stoop	toothpaste	thing	moonlight
roost	understood	tank	blanket
zinc	recognize	tents	scientist
crab	celebration	stand	instead

Lesson 38

Lesson Objectives

1. Students will review synonyms and antonyms. (L)
2. Students will review helping verbs. (L)
3. Students will review irregular nouns. (L)
4. Students will review the spelling list. (S)
5. Students will use clues to write spelling words. (S)
6. Students will copy sentences neatly and correctly. (H)

Materials

LAR Workbook page 43
SAP pages 35 and 36

Teaching

1. Use part 1 of LAR workbook page 43. **Read the word in bold print. Is the next word a synonym or antonym of the word in bold print? Fill in the correct circle.**
2. Use part 2 of LAR workbook page 43. **Read the sentences. A helping verb is needed. Rewrite the sentences with the correct helping verb for each tense.**
3. Review irregular nouns. Say the following words and ask if the noun is the plural form, singular form, or both: **Foot, teeth, sheep, man, reindeer, children.**
4. Use SAP page 35. **Unscramble the spelling words on the top part. Complete the sentences using spelling words that rhyme with the last word in the first line.**
5. Use SAP page 36. **Use the clues to write the spelling words.**
6. Use the handwriting sheet or have the children write the following sentences:

   The bloodhound recognized the scent.

   The rain drenched the blanket.

Lesson 38

LAR Answers

Part 1

1. antonym
2. antonym
3. synonym
4. synonym
5. antonym

Part 2

1. past tense: The kangaroo rat was hopping.
   present tense: The kangaroo rat is hopping.
2. past tense: The doughnuts were cooling off.
   present tense: The doughnuts are cooling off.
3. past tense: I was writing a story.
   present tense: I am writing a story.

SAP Answers page 35

Unscrambled words:

instead	
blanket	
drenched	automobile
bloodhound	doughnut
scientist	frighten

Rhymes:

moonlight	photograph
toothpaste	disappear
recognize	understood
everything	celebration

SAP Answers page 36

Use the clues to find the spelling words. A list is in the orange box.

frighten drenched blanket photograph instead celebration
toothpaste disappear everything recognize scientist
automobile doughnut understood moonlight bloodhound

It comes from a camera.
photograph

toothpaste

It means "move by itself".
automobile

It has a hole but doesn't go flat.
doughnut

A birthday party
celebration

It's on a bed.
blanket

A reflection of the sun
moonlight

It chases animals.
bloodhound

Soaking wet
drenched

A different choice
instead

Scare
frighten

Not seen anymore
disappear

All
everything

recognize

Know what was said
understood

This person makes discoveries.
scientist

Test 1
Lessons 39-40

Lesson Objectives

1. Students will take a test.

Materials

Test 1

Test Directions

The test can be given over a two-day period. Determining where to break is left to the discretion of the teacher.

Scoring: There are a total of 50 items, not counting the spelling test. Multiply the total correct by 2 for a percentage score, except part 6 where you multiply by four instead. Score spelling separately.

Part 1: Parts of speech

Read the sentences. Find the word that tells each part of speech. Write the words on the lines.

Part 2: Helping Verbs

Read the sentences. A helping verb is missing. Write a missing word for each tense. Write the helping verbs on the lines after the word past tense and present tense.

Part 3: Past and Present Tense

Read the sentences. Does the verb have the past of present tense? Fill in the circle.

Part 4: Synonyms and Antonyms

Read the pairs of words. Are they synonyms or antonyms? Fill in the correct circles.

Part 5: Irregular Nouns

Write a word that means more than one of each word. Write the plural form of each word. These are irregular nouns so you can't just add s.

Part 6: Comprehension and Inferences

Read the story. Answer the questions.

Part 7: Vocabulary

Match the words to the definitions. Write the letters next to the definitions in the boxes.

Spelling Test

Students will need paper for the test.

1. recognize, 2. scientist, 3. automobile, 4. frighten, 5. drenched, 6. blanket, 7. doughnut, 8. understood, 9. photograph, 10. instead, 11. celebration, 12. toothpaste, 13. disappear, 14. everything, 15. moonlight, 16. bloodhound

Test 1 Answers

Part 1

1. noun, park — pronoun, I — adjective, new
   verb, running — helping verb, am
2. noun, mouse — pronoun, It — adjective, brown
   verb, stalked — adverb, quietly

Part 2

1. past tense, was — present tense, is
2. past tense, were — present tense, are
3. present tense, am

Part 3

1. ● past ❍ present
2. ● past ❍ present
3. ❍ past ● present
4. ❍ past ● present
5. ❍ past ● present

Part 4

1. ● synonym ❍ antonym
2. ❍ synonym ● antonym
3. ● synonym ❍ antonym
4. ● synonym ❍ antonym
5. ❍ synonym ● antonym

Part 5

1. deer
2. teeth
3. wolves
4. feet
5. mice

Part 6

1. A. cold
2. D. rabbit
3. C. afternoon
4. B. Spring
5. C. deer

Part 7

1. E
2. G
3. D
4. A
5. I
6. F
7. B
8. J
9. C
10. H

Lesson 41

Lesson Objectives

1. Students will read and spell short vowel words. (P & S)
2. Students will learn vocabulary words. (L)
3. Students will begin reading the story *The Sky's the Limit*. (R)
4. Students will copy sentences neatly and correctly. (H)

Materials

SAP Workbook page 37
LAR Workbook pages 44
Book: *My Shoes Got the Blues* - Story 2: *The Sky's the Limit*

Teaching

1. Ask students to say the five short vowel sounds. Write the following words: volcanic, transmit, relapse, supposed, subway. Have students look at the vowels in the words. **Which vowels in each word make the short sound?** (volcanic, transmit, relapse, supposed, subway)

   Use the top of SAP page 37. **Look at the words in the box. They all have short vowel sounds. Alphabetize the spelling words. Write the words on the lines.** Use the bottom part of SAP workbook page 33. **Circle all the vowels that make the short sound.**

2. Introduce the vocabulary words for the story *The Sky's The Limit*.

   advertisement, allowance, autograph, contestant, decision, distracted,
   idol, imaginary, jealous, nervous, secretary

   Have students read the words and definitions on LAR workbook page 44. Answer the questions. Students may use the workbook page to help find the answers. Students may answer orally, or you may have them write the answers. The answers will be vocabulary words.

3. Introduce the story. Have students look at the table of contents in the book, *My Shoes Got the Blues* and find the story, *The Sky's The Limit*. Have students read the chapter titles for this story (chapters 1 to 5). Ask students to guess what they think the story might be about.

   Tell students that this is another story about Matthew Day. Ask students what they remember about the other stories featuring Matthew Day.

   Students will read chapter 1.

4. Use the handwriting sheet or have the children write the following sentences:

   The wagon was brimming with lemons.
   The insect landed on a cactus.

LAR Answers

jealous and nervous

contestant

advertisement

allowance

distracted

autograph

secretary

imaginary

SAP Answers

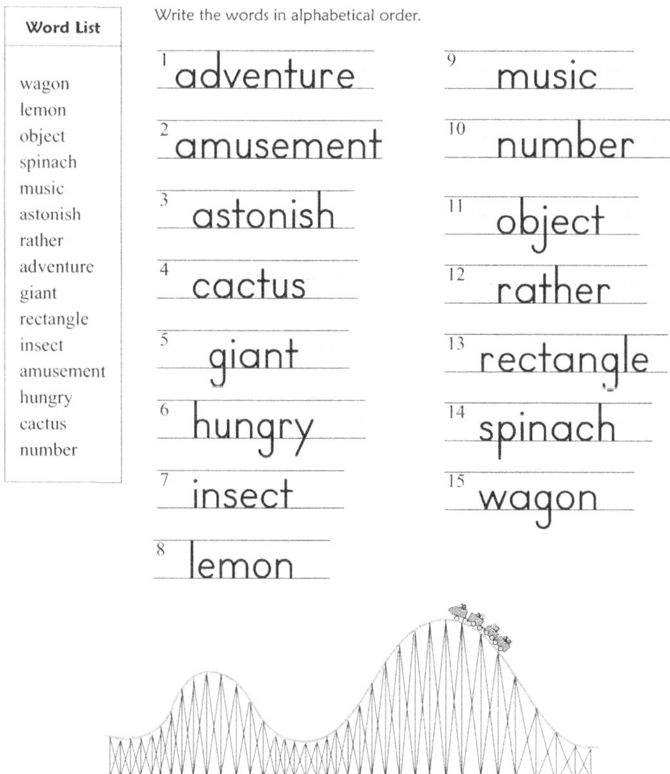

Word List
wagon
lemon
object
spinach
music
astonish
rather
adventure
giant
rectangle
insect
amusement
hungry
cactus
number

Write the words in alphabetical order.

1. adventure
2. amusement
3. astonish
4. cactus
5. giant
6. hungry
7. insect
8. lemon
9. music
10. number
11. object
12. rather
13. rectangle
14. spinach
15. wagon

Read the words. Circle any vowels that make a short sound.

1. giant 2. product 3. suggest 4. cabin 5. gigantic

Lesson 42

Lesson Objectives

1. Students will review short vowel sounds. (P)
2. Students will identify prepositions. (L)
3. Students will review spelling words. (S)
4. Students will read the story *The Sky's the Limit*. (R)
5. Students will copy sentences neatly and correctly. (H)
6. Students will consider the 5 senses in writing. (W)

Materials

LAR Workbook page 45
SAP Workbook page 38
WSW pages 21 and 22
Book: *My Shoes Got the Blues* - Story 2: *The Sky's the Limit*

Teaching

1. Part 1 of LAR workbook page 45. Have students choose a word from list A and add a word from list B to form words that fit the definitions.

   For example: Rabbit food. Combine the words *car* and *rot* for carrot.

2. **Prepositions are words that show a relationship between nouns or pronouns and some other word in a sentence.**

   Common prepositions are: about, above, across, after, against, along, among, around, at, before, behind, below, beneath, beside, between, beyond, by, down, during, except, for, from, in, into, like, near, of, off, on, onto, over, past, since, through, throughout, to, toward, under, underneath, until, unto, up, upon, with, within, without

   Introduce the term *preposition* and dictate some of the words in the list above. Next have students write sentences using some of the prepositions that you dictated.

   Part 2 of LAR workbook page 45: Read the sentences. Find the preposition. Write each sentence with a different preposition from the list.

   After completing the Part 2, ask students how changing the prepositions changed the meanings of the sentences.

3. Use SAP workbook page 38. **Fill in the boxes to write spelling words. One clue has been given for you. Start with the column that has a letter e in one of the boxes. Count the number of boxes in the column to know how many letters are in the word. Write the word that fills in the boxes.** (adventure) **Use the letters from this word for clues for more words that share boxes.**

4. Have students read chapter 2 of *The Sky's The Limit*. Ask these questions about chapters 1 & 2:

   What did Matthew win? (tickets to a Stingrays basketball game)
   Who do you think Sky Bordon is? (a basketball star)
   Where was Mr. Day going to drive Matthew? (to the radio station)

5. Use the handwriting sheet or have the children write the following sentences:

   Is the music playing in the carriage?
   Did the tailor mend the noblemen's coats?

6. Students will read the *Writing for the Senses* page. Students will add to each list. Students may use resources to add to the lists. Suggest search terms such as *words that describe senses*. On the next page, students will describe an amusement park using senses. If students have never been to an amusement park, they can imagine what it would be like.

   For example:

   There were shops to buy gifts lit with colorful, bright lights.

   The cars on the roller clanked as it climbed upward.

LAR Answers

Part 1

1. sunset
2. cabin
3. insect
4. hidden
5. wagon

Part 2

Answers vary.

SAP Answers

Fill in the boxes to make spelling words.

pdphoto.org public domain

wagon lemon object spinach music astonish
rather adventure giant rectangle insect
amusement hungry cactus number

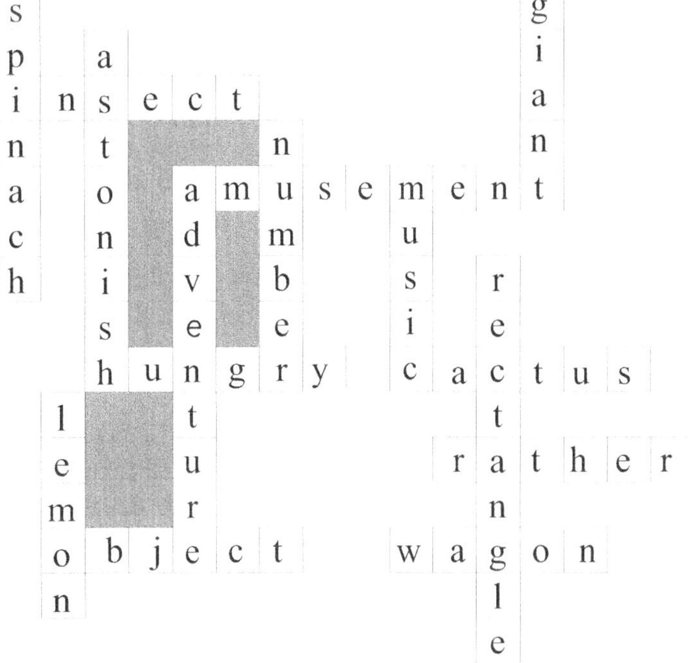

Lesson 43

Lesson Objectives

1. Students will determine fact from opinion. (L)
2. Students will review the spelling list. (S)
3. Students will read part of the story *The Sky's the Limit.* (R)
4. Students will copy sentences neatly and correctly. (H)
5. Students will write about insects in three different ways. (W)

Materials

LAR Workbook page 46
SAP Workbook page 39
WSW page 23
Book: *My Shoes Got the Blues* - Story 2: *The Sky's the Limit*

Teaching

1. Talk about facts and opinions. **A fact is something that is true. It's something that can be proved. It is something that is certain. An opinion is something that someone believes, thinks, or feels, but it cannot be proven.**

   Read the sentence: **The car has tires. Is that a fact or an opinion?** (It is a fact.) **You can prove the car has tires by looking at it.** Read the sentence: **Peanut butter tastes good. Is that a fact or an opinion?** (It is an opinion.) **It is an opinion because it is the way someone feels about the taste of peanut butter. Some people may not like peanut butter, so the sentence wouldn't be true for them.**

   Have students read the paragraphs on LAR workbook page 46. Students should then read the statements at the bottom of the page and fill in the circle. Is the statement a fact or an opinion?

2. Use SAP workbook page 39. Have students write spelling words to answer the questions or match the descriptions.

3. Ask the students the following questions about chapter 2. Then begin reading chapter 3.

   What was Joy Hansen talking about on the phone? (a promise Sky had made)
   What was the promise? (to be a part of a contest)
   Why do you think Sky didn't want to keep his promise? (Answers vary.)

4. Use the handwriting sheet or have the children write the following sentences:

   The giant astonished Jack.
   The cobbler fixed the red shoe.

5. Students will research and write about sentences. Students will first write facts on the green lines. The list of facts to research are suggestions of facts for students to explore. The blue lines are for a personal narrative about insects. Students will write about an experience they had with insects. The red lines are for writing an opinion about insects.

LAR Answers

1. ● fact ❍ opinion
2. ● fact ❍ opinion
3. ❍ fact ● opinion
4. ❍ fact ● opinion
5. ● fact ❍ opinion
6. ❍ fact ● opinion
7. ● fact ❍ opinion
8. ● fact ❍ opinion
9. ❍ fact ● opinion
10. ❍ fact ● opinion

SAP Answers

1. spinach
2. music
3. numbers
4. hungry
5. insect
6. astonish
7. giant
8. amusement
9. cactus
10. rectangle
11. wagon
12. adventure
13. lemon
14. object
15. rather

Lesson 44

Lesson Objectives

1. Students will describe how words are alike. (L)
2. Students will review spelling words. (S)
3. Students will read the story *The Sky's the Limit.* (R)
4. Students will write a story. (CW)
5. Students will copy sentences neatly and correctly. (H)

Materials

LAR Workbook page 47
SAP Workbook page 40
Book: *My Shoes Got the Blues* - Story 2: *The Sky's the Limit*

Teaching

1. Say the words: **cactus, sand, snakes. How are all of these things alike or what do they have in common?** (You can find them all in the desert.)

   Say these words: **tongue, wheels, axle. Use a spelling word to tell how these three things are alike.** (They are parts of a wagon.)

   Use LAR workbook page 47. **Write a sentence telling how the words in each list are alike. Use a spelling word. The spelling list is at the bottom of the page.**

2. Use the top of the SAP workbook page. **You've matched short words to spelling words that have the letters to spell the words in other lessons. Today, you'll match more than one spelling word to each short word. Look at the workbook page. The first word is *ant.* What letters are in the word *ant?*** (a-n-t) **Find all the spelling words that have an *a*, an *n*, and a *t*. The spelling words are in the box. The words are numbered. Write the number for the words that have all the letters in the small word. There are three blanks, so look for three words.** (6, 8, 9, 10, 12)

   Find the matches for the other words. You will use the numbers more than once.

   On the bottom section of the page, read the two sentences. Find the misspelled words and spell them correctly.

3. Ask questions about chapter 3.

   How do you think Matthew's father felt as they drove home from the radio station? (upset, angry, jealous)
   What things in the story help you realize how Mr. Day felt?
   (He gritted his teeth and stared at the road.)
   Why didn't Matthew want to play with his dad?
   (He was too excited about Sky Bordon.)
   Who won the basketball game between Mr. and Mrs. Day? (Mrs. Day)
   How do you know? (The loser fixed supper and Mr. Day cooked.)
   Have you ever been excited about a star like Sky Bordon?
   What do you think will happen next in the story? (Answers vary)

   Students will now read chapter 4 of the story *The Sky's The Limit.*

4. **What would it be like to be a superstar? How would you handle all the attention? Would it be a good thing if people made you an idol? Pretend that you are a superstar at something you like to do. Write a story about it.**

5. Use the handwriting sheet or have the children write the following sentences:

   I would rather ride in the wagon.
   Six is my favorite number.

LAR Answers

(Wording my vary - the key spelling word is in bold.)
1. They make **music**.
2. They are **insects**.
3. They are parts of a **lemon**.
4. They are **numbers**.
5. They are things to ride at an **amusement** park.

SAP Answers

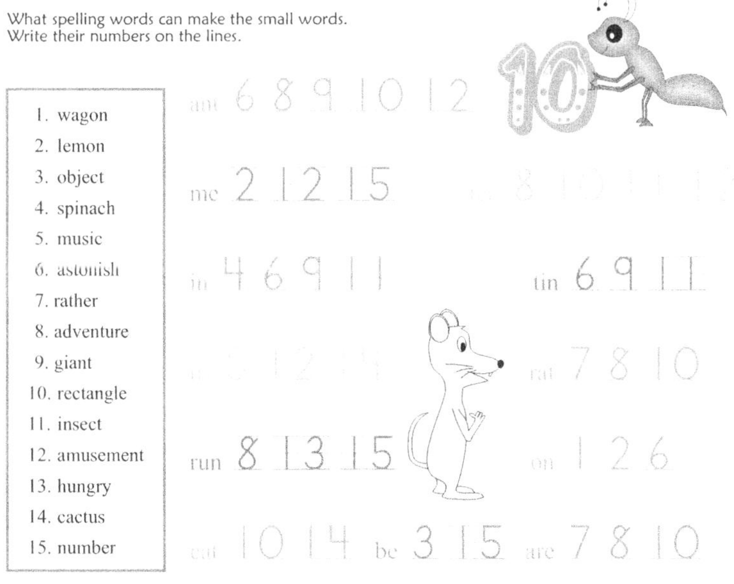

Find the misspelled spelling words. Write them correctly on the lines.

The musik at the amusment park came from inside the gient inesect.

The fresh leman smell made me hungrey.

Lesson 45

Lesson Objectives

1. Students will answer questions about the story *The Sky's The Limit.* (L)
2. Students will take a spelling test. (S)
3. Students will find the main idea of paragraphs. (L)
4. Students will read the stories they have written. (R)
5. Students will finish reading *The Sky's The Limit.* (R)
6. Students will copy sentences neatly and correctly. (H)

Materials

Creative writing assignment
Book: *My Shoes Got the Blues* - Story 2: *The Sky's the Limit*
LAR Workbook page 48

Teaching

1. Students will answer the following questions about the story. Use part 1 of LAR workbook page 48.

2. Have students number their paper from 1 to 15. Give the following words as dictation.

    1. rather, 2. music, 3. giant, 4. object, 5. insect, 6. adventure, 7. astonish, 8. lemon, 9. amusement, 10. cactus, 11. hungry, 12. spinach, 13. rectangle, 14. number, 15. wagon

3. **When we read a paragraph, there is usually one main idea that can be stated as a sentence.** Read the following paragraph and have students pick the sentence that tells the main idea.

    My dog Ruff chased a cat up the tree. The next day, he chased a squirrel up the tree. Ruff is very happy when he chases small animals. He almost caught a rabbit today.

    What is the main idea? A) Ruff chases cats. B) Ruff likes to chase small animals. C) Ruff likes to eat rabbits.

    Have students choose the correct answer (B). Discuss the different choices. A) is not the main idea because the paragraph doesn't just talk about cats. The same is true for rabbits in choice C). Answer B) describes the whole paragraph. It is the main idea.

    Part 2, LAR workbook page 48: **Read the sentences. Choose the main idea for each paragraph. Fill in the circle next to the correct answer.**

4. Have students read stories from the lesson 44 creative writing assignment.

5. Ask questions about chapter 4.

    What did Matthew have to do in the contest? (make the most baskets)
    How did Mack act like a bad sport? (He got angry when he missed. He didn't take turns.)
    Why did Ida wink at Matthew? (She missed on purpose.)
    What was the prize in the contest? (a day with Sky Bordon)
    How do you think Matthew's father felt? (Answers vary. He was jealous.)
    How do you know this? (Answers vary. He didn't want to go with Matthew and Sky.)

    Students will finish reading the story *The Sky's the Limit.* Have students read chapter 5.

6. Use the handwriting sheet or have the children write the following sentences:

   We were told to guard the red object.
   I am hungry for lemon pie.

LAR Answers

Part 1

Answers will vary.
Suggested answers:

1. Matthew wanted to meet Sky Bordon.
2. Matthew learned to not worship people.
3. Sky made shoes with blue soles.

Part 2

1. C
2. B

Lesson 46

Lesson Objectives

1. Students will review different spellings of the long oo. (P)
2. Students will spell words correctly. (S)
3. Students will use the prefixes un and re. (L)
4. Students will learn vocabulary words. (L)
5. Students will begin reading the story *Sole Winning*. (R)
6. Students will copy sentences neatly and correctly. (H)

Materials

LAR Workbook page 49
SAP Workbook page 41
Book: *My Shoes Got the Blues* - Story 3: *Sole Winning*

Teaching

1. Write the words mule and tulip. **Read the two words. The long u sound in mule sounds like the word "you". The "y" sound is dropped if the u comes after certain consonants (such as d, s, l, n, t). The long u sound with the "y" dropped is referred to as the long oo sound.**

   In the word tulip the u makes the long "oo" sound as in boot. This lesson will deal with the long oo sound spelled with vowel digraphs other than oo.

   Can you think of other ways they have spelled the "oo" sound in boot? (ew - flew, ue - blue, oe - shoe, ou – soup, ough-through). The digraph eu can also make the "oo" sound as in neutral, although most of these words are not used in the third grade, so "eu" words will not be included in exercises.

   Part 1 of LAR workbook page 49: **Read the descriptions. Write a long *oo* word that matches the description.** Students are given a word list: canoe, coupon, screwdriver, barbecue, jewelry, pursue, cougar.

2. Use the SAP workbook page. **Look at the spelling words. How are they all alike?** (They all have the long oo sound.) **Alphabetize the spelling words on the top part. The bottom section has four spelling words.**

   Take off part of each word to make another long *oo* word. Write the words *rescue* and *tourist*. **Don't mix up any of the letters, just take letters off. If you take the r-e-s off of the word *rescue* what word do you spell?** (cue) **If you take i-s-t off of the word *tourist* what word do you spell?** (tour) **Do the same with the words at the bottom of the workbook page.**

3. Students will use the prefixes re- and un-. Ask students if they know what a suffix is. Review common suffixes (such as –ing and –ed). **If suffixes come at the end of words, where do you think prefixes come?** (beginning) **Letters added to the beginning of words are prefixes. Two prefixes are r-e and u-n.**

   Tell students that e in re usually makes the long e sound and sometimes makes the short i sound. The u in un makes the short u sound. Have students think of words that begin with the prefixes re and un.

   (continued)

Have students compare words with and without the prefixes. For example, start and restart. How are the meanings of the words different? How did the prefix change the meaning? Try the words cover and uncover. How did the prefix un change the meaning of the word cover?

4. Introduce the vocabulary words for the story *Sole Winning*.

determined, immediately, important, impossible, ordinarily, responsible, stopwatch

Have students read the words and definitions on LAR workbook page 49.

Ask the following questions. Students may use the workbook page to help find the answers. Students may answer orally, or you may have them write the answers. The answers will be vocabulary words.

If you were told to do something right now, you would do it ____________. (immediately)
If you wanted to time something, you could use this. (stopwatch)
Something that you normally do is something that you ___________ do. (ordinarily)
Something that is really needed is this. (important)
If you don't give up, you are this. (determined)
Something that can't be done is this. (impossible)
If you are in charge, you are this. (responsible)

5. Introduce the story. Have students look at the table of contents and read the titles of the chapters. Have students guess what they think the story is about. Students will begin reading chapter 1 of the book, *My Shoes Got the Blues*, which is the first chapter of the story, *Sole Winning*.

6. Use the handwriting sheet or have the children write the following sentences:

The newspaper was full of advertisements.
We rescued the tourist in the canoe.

LAR Answers

Part 1

1. cougar
2. barbecue
3. coupon
4. pursue
5. canoe
6. screwdriver
7. jewelry

Part 2

reading only

SAP Answers

Word List

nephew
review
newspaper
avenue
continue
rescue
shoestring
canoe
through
caribou
tourist
youth
costume
include
student

Write the words in alphabetical order.

1 avenue
2 canoe
3 caribou
4 continue
5 costume
6 include
7 nephew
8 newspaper
9 rescue
10 review
11 shoestring
12 student
13 through
14 tourist
15 youth

Take letters away from these words to make other words with the long oo sound.

review view
shoestring shoe
youth you
newspaper new or news

Lesson 47

Lesson Objectives

1. Students will review long oo. (P)
2. Students will review plural nouns. (L)
3. Students will review spelling words. (S)
4. Students will read the story *Sole Winning*. (R)
5. Students will copy sentences neatly and correctly. (H)
6. Students will describe a costume. (W)

Materials

LAR Workbook page 50
SAP Workbook page 42
WSW pages 24 and 25
Book: *My Shoes Got the Blues* - Story 3: *Sole Winning*

Teaching

1. Review the different ways the long oo sound can be spelled instead of oo. (ew, ue, oe, ou, ough, u and silent e)

   Part 1 of LAR workbook page 50: Read the sentences. Find and circle the words that have the long oo sound.

2. Ask students to give simple definitions for the term noun. (A noun is a person, place, or thing) Ask students to name some nouns. Write the words rabbit and rabbits. **How are the words different?** (rabbits means more than one rabbit.) **What do we call the form of a noun that means more than one?** (plural)

   How does the spelling of nouns change when we write the plural form of words that end with y? Use the word *bunny* for an example. (bunnies) Review the rule to drop the y and add -ies.

   Part 2 of LAR workbook page 50: **Read the nouns. Write the plural forms. Then write a sentence using the plural form of the word.**

3. Use SAP page 42. **Look at the top of the workbook page. The spelling word is numbered. Small words are listed with sets of lines. What spelling words have the letters to make the small words? The first word is *use*. What words have a u, s, and an e? Write their numbers on the lines. Repeat with the other words.**

   In the bottom section, sort the words by the way the long oo sound is spelled.

4. Ask these questions about chapter 1 of *Sole Winning* and begin reading chapter 2.

   How did Matthew wake up in the morning? (Buster pulled the blanket off the bed.)
   What was missing from his room? (His shoe.)
   What do you think happened to it? (Answers vary.)
   Why was finding the shoe so important to Matthew? (He wanted to beat Buzz in a race.)
   How did Matthew feel about Buzz? Why do you think he felt that way?
   What do you think "snail boy" means?

5. Use the handwriting sheet or have the children write the following sentences:

   The students were very nervous.
   They were reviewing for the big test.

6. Students will design and write about a costume. Students will write an overall description. They will list the materials used in the costume. Students will write about their expectations of others who see the costume. Students will list steps it would take to make the costume. Students should use words that show order such as first, second, next, and last. Students will draw the costume on the next page.

   Note: Students can also make illustrations on another piece of paper for any stories or research papers they create. In this case, the drawing space was included to format pages 26 and 27 so both pages could be viewed at one time.

LAR Answers

Part 1

1. My (new) (shoes) are covered with (blue) (goo).
2. Is (Bruce) (through) eating the (soup)?
3. (You) should (choose) to (chew) beefy (stew).
4. The boy (threw) the (newspaper) on the (roof).
5. The toy (canoe) was (Sue's) (souvenir).

Part 2
Answers vary for sentences.

plurals
1. babies
2. families
3. countries

SAP Answers

1. nephew
2. review
3. newspaper
4. avenue
5. continue
6. rescue
7. shoestring
8. canoe
9. through
10. caribou
11. tourist
12. youth
13. costume
14. include
15. student

What spelling words can make the small words.
Write their numbers on the lines.

use 6 13 15
hot 7 9 12
to 5 7 9 11 12 13
or 7 9 10 11
an 3 4 8
rot 7 9 11
hen 1 7
ice 5 14
we 1 2 3
no 5 7 8

Sort the words by the way the oo sound is spelled.

ew
nephew
review
newspaper

ou
caribou
tourist
youth

avenue
continue
rescue

u-consonant-e
costume
include
student

ough
through

oe
shoestring
canoe

Lesson 48

Lesson Objectives

1. Students will describe how words are alike (categories). (L)
2. Students will add suffixes to spelling words. (S)
3. Students will review vocabulary words. (L)
4. Students will read part of the story, *Sole Winning*. (R)
5. Students will copy sentences neatly and correctly. (H)
6. Students will research and write about caribou.

Materials

LAR Workbook page 51
SAP Workbook page 43
WSW pages 26 and 27
Book: *My Shoes Got the Blues* - Story 3: *Sole Winning*

Teaching

1. Write the words medal, trophy, and ribbon. Ask students to tell how these words are alike. (ex. You win them.) Next, have students describe how they are alike using the word contestants. (something contestants can win)

   Part 1 of workbook page 51: Have students use the key word to write a sentence telling how the words in bold print are alike.

2. Use the SAP page to review spelling rules for adding suffixes. **Add suffixes to the words. Remember what to do with silent e. Add words to the two sentences. Add suffixes to the words above the lines.**

3. Students will need a piece of paper with lines numbered from 1 to 7. **I will read a sentence. Listen for the vocabulary word. Write the vocabulary word on your paper.**

   1. **The lifeguard *immediately* jumped into the swimming pool.**
   2. **The coach used a *stopwatch* to time the race.**
   3. **Who is *responsible* for the mess in the bathroom?**
   4. **The angry bull was *determined* to get out of the pen.**
   5. **It was *impossible* to swim across the flooded river.**
   6. ***Ordinarily*, the river wasn't very deep.**
   7. **It is *important* that you tell your parents where you are going.**

4. Ask the questions about chapter 2 of *Sole Winning* and begin reading chapter 3.

   Where did Matthew leave his shoes the night before? (at the front door)
   Who brought them to Matthew's room? (Rachel)
   How did she describe the shoes? (stinky)
   What do you think happened to the shoe?
   What did Matthew's mom promise to do? (She promised to find the shoe and bring it to school.)

5. Use the handwriting sheet or have the children write the following sentences:

   I will buy a costume with my allowance.
   I will be a contestant in the spelling bee.

6. Students will research to answer the questions about caribou. Students will then write a story about having a caribou for a pet. Students should include some caribou facts in their stories.

LAR Answers

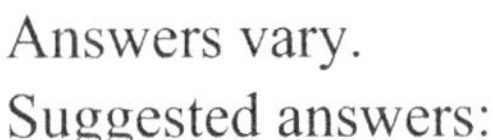
Answers vary.
Suggested answers:

1. These are things a secretary does.
2. They are decisions to make.
3. These are people who give autographs.
4. These are places to look for information.
5. They are things people wear as costumes.

SAP Answers

The suffixes *er* and *ed* can be added to words to change the way they are used in sentences.

If a word ends with a silent e, drop the silent e before adding a suffix beginning with a vowel. blue bluer

Add the suffixes to these words:

review + er	continue + ed	rescue + ing
reviewer	continued	rescuing
costume + ed	**rescue + er**	**include + ing**
costumed	rescuer	including

If a word ends with oe, the e is dropped when adding ed or er. The e is not dropped if adding ing. shoe shoed shoeing

Add the suffixes to the word canoe:

canoe + ed	canoe + er	canoe + ing
canoed	canoer	canoeing

Add a suffix to the word above the lines to complete the sentence.

canoe

We enjoy canoeing on the lake.

rescue

The fireman rescued the cat stuck in the tree.

Lesson 49

Lesson Objectives

1. Students will combine sentences. (L)
2. Students will review spelling words. (S)
3. Students will read the story *Sole Winning*. (R)
4. Students will write a story. (CW)
5. Students will copy sentences neatly and correctly. (H)

Materials

LAR Workbook page 52
SAP Workbook page 44
Book: *My Shoes Got the Blues* - Story 3: *Sole Winning*

Teaching

1. Tell the students: **When authors write books for children, they must be easier to read. One way to do this is to use shorter sentences. Now that you are better readers, you can read longer sentences.**

   Write the following two sentences:

   The puppy was very cute. It was brown and white.

   We can make these two sentences into one sentence. Look at the second sentence. What does it tell us about the puppy? (It was brown and white.)

   That's the only thing new the second sentence tells us. If we can put the words brown and white into the first sentence, we wouldn't need the second sentence. Before what word can we put the words *brown* and *white*? (puppy) **What is the new sentence?** The brown and white puppy was very cute. **You could also say the very cute puppy was brown and white.**

   Students will combine two sentences into one. **Combine these two sentences:**

   I have lots of toys. They are in my closet. Answer: (I have lots of toys in my closet)

   Use LAR workbook page 52. **Combine the two sentences and write them on the workbook page.** If you need to, point out the place to insert the key words from the second sentence (like before the word *puppy* in the example).

2. Use the SAP page. **Write the spelling word that matches the description.**

3. Ask these questions about chapter 3 of *Sole Winning* and begin reading chapter 4.

   Why did Matthew think he ran so slowly? (He had the wrong shoes.)
   Rachel accused Matthew of hiding the shoe. Why did she think he hid the shoe? (So he would have an excuse to lose.)
   Where did Mrs. Day find the shoe? (In Buster's dog house.)

   How did the shoe get there? (Buster took it.) **When did the pup take it?** (After he pulled the blanket off of Matthew.)
   How do you think Matthew will feel when he gets his shoes?

4. **Have you ever been in a race or some other kind of contest? If you have, write a story based on your experience. If not, imagine what it would be like. Writers often use their own experiences to develop a story. They then add or change things to make it even more fun or interesting. It's okay to use your imagination along with your experiences to create a new story.**

   This is called fiction. It's a story that didn't really happen. The reader usually knows it didn't happen, even though it could be possible that the story might have happened. Use different characters in the story, rather than yourself, to help the reader understand that this is a fictional story.

5. Use the handwriting sheet or have the children write the following sentences:

   The cougar distracted the caribou.
   The secretary tied her shoestring.

LAR Answers

Example answers (wording may vary)

1. The caribou with large antlers grazed in the meadow.
2. I got a new, blue bike.
3. The zoo has a new tiger from India.
4. I will go to the store to get peanut butter.
5. We rode in a leaky canoe.
6. The cat climbed a tall tree.

SAP Answers

nephew review newspaper avenue continue rescue shoestring canoe through caribou tourist youth costume include student

To look over again
review

caribou

It's someone in school.
student

Keep going
continue

A visitor
tourist

To save
rescue

In one end, out the other
through

Opposite of exclude
include

A disguise
costume

Read it to learn what happened.
newspaper

Street
avenue

A brother's son
nephew

Tie it or trip on it.
shoestring

youth

A boat
canoe

Lesson 50

Lesson Objectives

1. Students will answer questions about the story *Sole Winning*. (L)
2. Students will take a spelling test. (S)
3. Students will read the stories they have written. (R)
4. Students will read the story, *Sole Winning*. (R)
5. Students will copy a sentence neatly and correctly. (H)

Materials

Creative writing assignment
LAR Workbook pages 53

Teaching

1. Use LAR workbook page 53. Answer the questions about the story.

2. Have students number their paper from 1 to 15. Give the following words as dictation.

   1. youth, 2. shoestring, 3. review, 4. caribou, 5. continue, 6. include, 7. canoe, 8. avenue, 9. costume, 10. through, 11. rescue, 12. student, 13. newspaper, 14. tourist, 15. nephew

3. Have students read stories from the lesson 49 creative writing assignment.

4. Ask questions about chapter 4 of *Soul Winning.*

   Why was Buzz late for school? (He had a dentist appointment.)
   What was Buzz's idea? (To wear Matt's Double Pump Slammers)
   Why do you think he did that? (answers vary)
   What do you think Matthew felt about Buzz when he saw the shoes?
   What would you say to Buzz at the end of the race?
   Do you think Matt can win with his old shoes?
   Read chapter 5 to find out.

5. Use the handwriting sheet or have the children write the following sentences:

   It is wrong to make people into idols.
   Our nephew was jealous of the other youth.

LAR Answers

Answers will vary.
Suggested answers:

1. Buster hid it.
2. He needed shoes for running.
3. He thought Buzz was cheating.
4. Friends are more important than things.

Lesson 51

Lesson Objectives

1. Students will review vowel digraphs ou and ow as in sound and cow. (P)
2. Students will spell words correctly. (S)
3. Students will practice dictionary skills. (L)
4. Students will learn vocabulary words. (L)
5. Students will begin reading the story *Tidbit and the Bell.* (R)
6. Students will copy sentences neatly and correctly. (H)

Materials

Dictionary
LAR Workbook page 54
SAP Workbook page 45
Book: *Tidbit and the Bell*

Teaching

1. Write the words cow and house. Have students read the two words. **What vowel sound do you hear in these words?** (*ou*) **What are two ways to spell the *ou* sound?** (ou and ow)

   Say the words mouse, tower, chow and couch. Ask students to decide how the ou sound is spelled in each word. In general:

   If a word ends with the ou sound, it is spelled ow.

   If the ou sound is immediately followed with a vowel, it is also usually spelled with an ow.

   If the ou sound is immediately followed with a consonant, it is also usually spelled with an ou.

   Have students take out a piece of paper. Give students three or four minutes to think of and write as many *ou* words as possible. You may make a game of it. Students will get one point for each word, a second point if the word was spelled correctly, and a bonus point for each word that no one else in the class thought of, or make your own list too and give a point for each word the students thought of that you didn't.

2. Use the SAP workbook page. **Look at the spelling words. How are they all alike?** (They all have the ow sound as in cow.) **What two ways are the *ow* sound spelled?** (ou and ow) **Sort the words by how the *ow* sound is spelled. One word has both ow and ou. It has its own box. Do the ow and ou make the same vowel sound?**

   One the bottom of the page take letters away from the spelling words to make other words.

3. Use the top of the LAR workbook page. **Find the following words in a dictionary: astound, devour, boundary, encounter, fowl, dowry, chowder, and endowment. They are printed on the workbook page.**

   Match the words to the descriptions. Write the number from the word list in front of the matching description.

4. Introduce the vocabulary words for the story *Tidbit and the Bell.* Students may look at the list at the bottom of the LAR workbook page.

   adventure, attention, commotion, complain, creature, daydream, encourage, introduced, refreshing, tremendous, trustworthy

   Read the words and definitions on the bottom of the LAR workbook page.

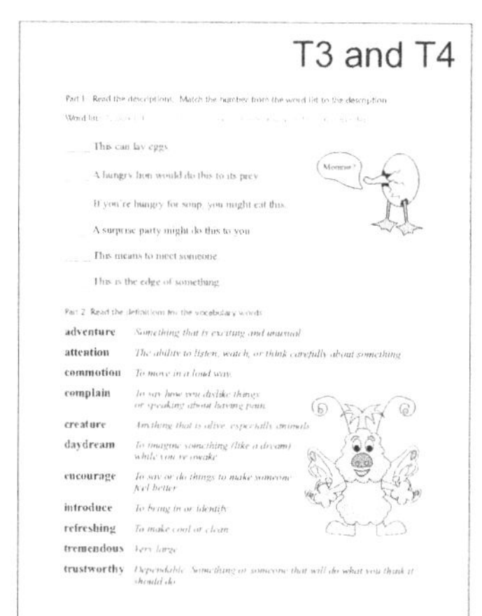
T3 and T4

Part 1 Read the descriptions. Match the number from the word list to the description.

___ This can lay eggs.

___ A hungry lion would do this to its prey.

___ If you're hungry for soup, you might eat this.

___ A surprise party might do this to you.

___ This means to meet someone.

___ This is the edge of something.

Part 2 Read the definitions for the vocabulary words.

adventure *Something that is exciting and unusual*

attention *The ability to listen, watch, or think carefully about something*

commotion *To move in a loud way*

complain *To say how you dislike things or speaking about having pain*

creature *Anything that is alive, especially animals*

daydream *To imagine something (like a dream) while you're awake*

encourage *To say or do things to make someone feel better*

introduce *To bring in or identify*

refreshing *To make cool or clean*

tremendous *Very large*

trustworthy *Dependable. Something or someone that will do what you think it should do*

5. Introduce the story. Have students look at the title page. Students should read the title and the description on the title page.

   This is a story is about a little mouse named Tidbit. It is the first of a series of three books that tell the story of Tidbit and his adventures.

   Students will begin reading the first chapter of *Tidbit and the Bell.*

6. Use the handwriting sheet or have the children write the following sentences:

   Climbing a mountain is an adventure.
   I dropped my brownie on the couch.

LAR Answers

Part 1

5
2
6
1
4
3

Part 2
reading only

SAP Answers

Word List
coward
mountain
thousand
eyebrow
counter
amount
flower
announce
couch
powder
shower
cloudy
brownie
downpour
flour
cowboy

Sort the words by how they are spelled.

ou	ow
mountain	coward
thousand	eyebrow
counter	flower
amount	powder
announce	shower
couch	brownie
cloudy	cowboy
flour	

both ou and ow downpour

Do ou and ow make the same sound? ○ yes ● no

Take letters away from these words to make other words with the ow sound as in *now.*

cloudy cloud or loud

announce noun or ounce

Take letters away from these words to make words with the long o sound as in *mow.*

flower flow, or low, or lower

shower show

Lesson 52

Lesson Objectives

1. Students will review ou and ow. (P)
2. Students will use verbs in past, present, and future tense. (L)
3. Students will find parts of spelling words. (S)
4. Students will add suffixes and prefixes to words. (S)
5. Students will read the story *Tidbit and the Bell.* (R)
6. Students will copy sentences neatly and correctly. (H)
7. Students will write opinion paragraphs. (W)

Materials

LAR Workbook page 55
SAP Workbook page 46
WSW pages 28 and 29
Book: *Tidbit and the Bell*

Teaching

1. Write the words ton, hose, and put. Ask students to add a letter (o, u, or w) to each word to make words that have the *ou* sound. (town, house, pout)

   LAR workbook part 1: Read the words. Add the letters o, u, or w to make words with the *ou* sound. Write the new words on the lines.

2. Ask students to give simple definitions for the term verb. (A verb is an action word. It tells what happens to the noun.) **Name some verbs.** Write the words ran and run. **How the words are different?** (The two words mean the same thing, the difference is the tense.) **Tense refers to when something happens.** Introduce the three tenses: past tense, present tense, and future tense. Write the sentences with the vowels underlined:

   1. We will run to the store.
   2. We ran to the store.
   3. We are running to the store.

   Ask the students: **Which sentence tells about running in the past (2), future (1), and present (3)?**

   Part 2 of the LAR workbook: **Read the sentences. Underline the verb and find its tense. Fill in the circle next to the words past, present, or future.**

3. Write the word *our.* Use the top of the SAP workbook. **Look at the spelling list on page 45. Find the spelling words that have o-u-r, *our,* as a part of the word.** (flour, downpour) **Do the letters make the same sound in each word? Find the spelling words that contain the words cow, mount, and brow. Write them on the lines.**

4. **What is a prefix?** (Letters added to the front of words.) **What is a suffix?** (Letters added to the end of words.) **The letters change the meaning of words or the way they are used in sentences.** Use the bottom of the SAP workbook page. **Match prefixes or suffixes to the spelling words in the box. Choose one of the new words you wrote and use it in a sentence on the black lines.** The vowel sound changes when -ish is added to flour.

   You may have students find the word in a dictionary and read the definition and pronunciation.

5. Ask these questions about chapter 1 of *Tidbit and the Bell*:

   Why did Tidbit like bells? (A bell had saved his father's life. He liked the sound.)
   How did a rat help Tidbit's father? (He hit a cat with a bell.)
   What was the rat's name? (Fritz Aldrich Rat)
   Describe the rat that Tidbit met in the entryway. (sharp teeth, wide mouth, long thin fingers, smelled like garbage)
   Why do you think Tidbit wanted the bell? (Answers vary.)
   Do you think Tidbit will get the bell from the rat? (Answers vary.)

   Now have students read chapter 2.

6. Use the handwriting sheet or have the children write the following sentences:

   The announcement caused a commotion.
   I daydreamed that I was a cowboy.

7. Students will begin by reading the Writing Opinion Paragraphs sheet. Students will learn a structure and tips for writing a persuasive paragraph. On the following page, students will write a persuasive paragraph. Students will make an argument from a choice of four sentences.

LAR Answers

Part 1

1. noun
2. mouse
3. now
4. found
5. down
6. sow
7. shout
8. spout
9. cloud
10. ounce

Part 2

1.	● past	❍ present	❍ future
2.	❍ past	● present	❍ future
3.	❍ past	● present	❍ future
4.	❍ past	● present	❍ future
5.	❍ past	❍ present	● future
6.	● past	❍ present	❍ future
7.	● past	❍ present	❍ future
8.	❍ past	❍ present	● future
9.	❍ past	❍ present	● future
10.	● past	❍ present	❍ future

SAP Answers

Find the spelling words that contain these smaller words.

brownie eyebrow
mountain amount
coward cowboy

Match the prefixes or suffixes to the spelling words. Write the new words. Use one of the words in a sentence on the black lines.

dis ish ous
ment y ly

mountain counter
announce powder
coward flour

Photo National Park Service public domain

discounter mountainous
announcement powdery
[illegible] flourish

Lesson 53

Lesson Objectives

1. Students will work with analogies. (L)
2. Students will review vocabulary words. (L)
3. Students will write an opinion paragraph. (W)
4. Students will review the spelling list. (S)
5. Students will read part of the story *Tidbit and the Bell.* (R)
6. Students will copy sentences neatly and correctly. (H)

Materials

LAR Workbook page 56
SAP Workbook page 47
WSW page 30
Book: *Tidbit and the Bell*

Teaching

1. Write the words boy and girl. **Are these words synonyms or opposites?** (opposites)

   Write the words wrench and bolt. **How are the words are related?** (You use a wrench to turn a bolt.)

   Next write the statement: boy is to girl as cool is to _________ (cold or warm)

   How do you know the answer isn't cold? (Because boy and girl are opposites. The opposite of cool is warm, not cold.)

   Next write the statement: Wrench is to bolt as hammer is to __________ (nail)
   Wrench and bolt are not opposites or synonyms. They are related by a purpose. A wrench is a tool used on a bolt. A hammer is a tool used on what? (a nail)

   These are called analogies. We look at the relationship between two words to decide how another pair of words fit together. The words boy and girl have the same relationship as the words cool and warm. They are both pairs of opposites.

   Wrench and bolt have a similar relationship as hammer and nail. Knowing the relationship to the first two words helps us decide the relationship of the last two words.

   Part 1 of the LAR workbook page: **Complete the analogies. Fill in the circle next to the correct word.** After students have completed the exercise, review the analogies, discussing the relationships between words.

2. Review the vocabulary words. Use the LAR workbook page. Have students read each word and state a brief definition. Students will complete the sentences on part 2 of the LAR workbook page using the vocabulary word list. Adventure, tremendous, and trustworthy were not used. Students may write their own sentences for these words on a piece of paper.

3. Students can refer back to the Writing Opinion Paragraphs page. Students will make an argument for the worse choice.

3. Have students write sentences using the spelling words.

   Pretty *flowers* grew on the *mountain*.
   The man with thick *eyebrows* is a *cowboy*.
   We need *flour* and *powdered* sugar to make *brownies*.
   The *coward* at the *counter* made the *announcement*.
   The *couch* costs a *thousand* dollars.
   A *shower* of rain fell from the *cloudy* skies.
   A *downpour* is a large *amount* of rain.

   Next, students will fill in the grid on the SAP workbook page with spelling words.

4. Finish reading the second chapter of *Tidbit and the Bell*. Ask the students the following questions then begin reading chapter 3.

   What were the two rats doing with the bell? (playing keep-away from the other rat)
   How did Tidbit move the bell? (He climbed on it and rolled it.)
   What problem did this cause? (It rolled into the two big rats.)
   What happened to the two big rats? (They ran into each other and knocked each other out.)
   The rat asked Tidbit if he could keep a secret. The rat liked Tidbit's answer. Why do you think the rat liked the answer? (Answers vary. He knew Tidbit was good and honest.)
   How does that make you feel about the rat? Do you think he is a good or bad rat?
   Do you think he is selfish for keeping the bell? Why or why not?
   Why did Tidbit follow the rat? (He wanted the bell.)
   Is it wise to go with a stranger? (no) **Why?**

5. Use the handwriting sheet or have the children write the following sentences:

   The shy creature hid behind the flowers.
   The white powder is flour.

LAR Answers

Part 1

1.	❍ child	● man	❍ girl
2.	❍ coat	❍ fruit	● dog
3.	● short	❍ high	❍ big
4.	❍ knife	❍ dirt	● eat
5.	❍ drive	● shoes	❍ round
6.	● run	❍ jump	❍ kick
7.	● pretty	❍ duckling	❍ angry

Part 2

1. refreshing
2. attention
3. commotion
4. complain
5. creature
6. encourage
7. introduced

SAP Answers

Fill in the boxes to make spelling words.

Across: announce, counter, cowboy, mountain, thousand, brownie, flower, powder, coward
Down: cloudy, couch, amount, downpour, eyebrow, shower, flour

mountain thousand counter cloudy
amount announce couch powder
coward shower flower brownie
downpour eyebrow flour cowboy

Lesson 54

Lesson Objectives

1. Students will review spelling words. (S)
2. Students will read the story *Tidbit and the Bell.* (R)
3. Students will write a story. (CW)
4. Students will copy sentences neatly and correctly. (H)

Materials

Book: *Tidbit and the Bell*
SAP Workbook page 48

Teaching

1. Use the SAP workbook page. **Write the spelling words that match the clues.**

2. Ask questions about chapter 3.

   Where was Tidbit when he woke up in the morning? (in a cage)
   Why didn't Tidbit want to stay in the cage? (He wanted to be free.)
   How do you think this made Tidbit feel about the rat? (Answers vary. Tidbit may have felt that the rat was not trustworthy.)
   Why do you think the mice wanted to help Tidbit take the bell? (Answers vary.)
   Why had the rat left Tidbit in the cage? (He had to fix the ladder. He wanted Tidbit to get some rest.)
   What do you think the rat will do next? (Answers vary.)

   Students will now read chapter four of the book *Tidbit and the Bell.*

3. **Tidbit was a very small mouse. Things that look small to us look big to Tidbit. He couldn't even lift the little brass bell. What do you think it would be like to be as small as a mouse? What things might scare you? What things would be harder or easier to do? What could you do that you can't do now? Write a story where you, or a character you make up, are as small as a mouse.**

4. Use the handwriting sheet or have the children write the following sentences:

   The shower was refreshing at first.
   It became a tremendous downpour.

SAP Answers

Use the clues to find the spelling words. A list is in the orange box.

mountain thousand counter cloudy
amount announce couch powder
coward shower flower brownie
downpour eyebrow flour cowboy

Afraid to do something

coward

Stand up bath

shower

thousand

A chocolate snack

brownie

Not sunny

cloudy

Hair

eyebrow

To tell news

announce

Rides a horse to work

cowboy

Tulip

flower

A heavy rain

downpour

A soft place to sit

couch

Used to make bread

flour

A tall rocky place

mountain

How much?

amount

counter

Like dust

powder

Lesson 55

Lesson Objectives

1. Students will answer questions about the story *Tidbit and the Bell.* (L)
2. Students will take a spelling test. (S)
3. Students will understand figurative language. (L)
4. Students will read the stories they have written. (R)
5. Students will copy a sentence neatly and correctly. (H)
6. Students will read and respond to fables. (R)

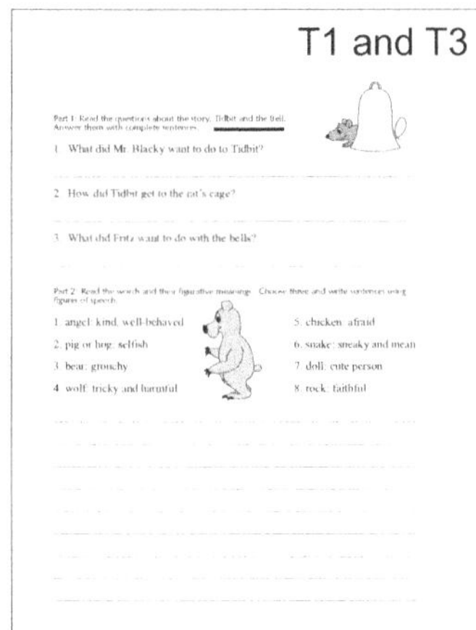
T1 and T3

Part 1: Read the questions about the story, Tidbit and the Bell. Answer them with complete sentences.

1. What did Mr. Blacky want to do to Tidbit?

2. How did Tidbit get to the rat's cage?

3. What did Fritz want to do with the bells?

Part 2: Read the words and their figurative meanings. Choose three and write sentences using figures of speech.

1. angel: kind, well-behaved
2. pig or hog: selfish
3. bear: grouchy
4. wolf: tricky and harmful
5. chicken: afraid
6. snake: sneaky and mean
7. doll: cute person
8. rock: faithful

Materials

Creative writing assignment
Book: *Tidbit and the Bell*
LAR Workbook page 57
Resource Pack Fable Sheet

Teaching

1. Use part 1 of the LAR workbook page. Answer the questions about the story.

2. Have students number their paper from 1 to 16. Give the following words as dictation.

   1. amount, 2. powder, 3. cowboy, 4. couch, 5. shower, 6. counter, 7. flower, 8. brownie, 9. announce, 10. eyebrow, 11. mountain, 12. downpour, 13. cloudy, 14. thousand, 15. coward, 16. flour

3. **In the story,** *Tidbit and the Bell,* **Fritz the rat says, "Most of the creatures I know are real rats." Find this on page 8 of your book. This sentence can have two meanings.**

   Fritz could mean that most of the creatures he knows are the animals called rats. Rat can have a different meaning in this sentence. If a person is called a rat, what do you think is meant by that? (Someone who can't be trusted.)

   In this part of the story, Fritz the Rat is trying to find out if Tidbit can keep a secret. So, Fritz might mean that the creatures he knows are not trustworthy, or he might mean that they are the animals called rats. Which do you think he means?

   When we use the word rat to describe someone who is not trustworthy, we are using a figure of speech. Writers do this to make writing more interesting. Figurative language helps us paint a picture in our minds. It gets the reader more involved in the writing. You can make your own writing more interesting by using figures of speech.

   Which sounds more interesting: "That boy is not trustworthy," ***or*** **"That boy is a real rat!"?**

   Use part 2 of the LAR workbook page. Have students read the words and figurative meanings. Students choose three words. Have students write three sentences using the figurative meanings.

   You may ask students to think of other figures of speech. Students may even create new ones.

4. Have students read stories from the lesson 54 creative writing assignment.

5. Use the handwriting sheet or have the children write the following sentences:

   A coward is not trustworthy.
   I didn't complain about the cloudy day.

6. Use the Fable Sheet. Students will read the fables *The Eagle and the Crow* and *The Kid and the Wolf.* Students will then write their opinion about which fable they liked best and why.

LAR Answers

Part 1

Answers will vary.
Suggested answers:

1. Mr. Blacky wanted to eat Tidbit.
2. He rode on a train.
3. He wanted to use the bells to warn rats and mice of danger.

Part 2

Answers vary.

Lesson 56

Lesson Objectives

1. Students will review the different sounds of the vowel digraph ea. (P)
2. Students will identify homophones. (L)
3. Students will spell words correctly. (S)
4. Students will learn vocabulary words. (L)
5. Students will begin reading the story *Tidbit to the Rescue*. (R)
6. Students will copy sentences neatly and correctly. (H)

Materials

SAP workbook page 49
LAR workbook page 58
Book: *Tidbit to the Rescue*

Teaching

1. Write the words peach, search, beauty, great, bread, wear. **What two vowels do all of these words have in common?** (ea) **In each of these words, the ea makes a different sound.**

   Have students identify the different sounds: peach – long e, search – er, beauty – long u (beauty and beautiful are the only words where ea helps make the long u sound), great- long a, bread- short e, wear- "air" sound.

   Teacher notes: ea can also make the "air" sound as in *bear*. Ea + r does not always make the –er sound. If the letter after the r is a vowel, the r moves to the next syllable such as in hearing and wearing. Another exception is the word *heart* (-ear has the –ar sound). In a few words with Latin roots, both letters retain their sounds as in *reality*. Some words depend on context. The word *read* can have the long or short e sound. These exceptions need not be taught at this time.

   Use the top part of the LAR workbook: **Read the sentences. Underline words that have the vowel digraph ea. Fill in the circle that tells if ea makes the short or long e sound.**

2. Write the words steel and steal. **How are the two words alike?** (They sound alike.) **How are they different?** (They have different meanings.) **Words that sound alike, but are spelled differently and have different meanings are called homophones. Spell the word that is a kind of metal.** (s-t-e-e-l) **What does the other word mean?** (to take something wrongfully)

   Use LAR workbook page 58 part 2. **Read the pairs of sentences. The words in bold print are homophones. The context of the words in the sentence gives clues to the meaning. Complete the definitions of each homophone by writing the correct number in the blank.**

3. Have the students look at the spelling words in the box on SAP page 45. **Look at the words in the box. How are they all alike?** (They all have the vowel digraph ea.) **Remember e-a makes several different sounds. Sort the words by the sounds the letters e-a make. Write the words on the lines. Write the root words of the two words at the bottom of the page. Take off the suffixes and change the spelling of the root if needed.**

   Spelling List: teacher, earthworm, season, pleasant, meaning, forehead, treasure, breakfast, increase, beautiful, steak, search, meadow, beagle

4. Introduce the vocabulary words for the story *Tidbit to the Rescue*. Students may look at the list on the first page of the story.

    Concerned, desperately, expand, explain, relief, unexpected

    Ask the students which word fits the definitions:

    Which word means:
    to become larger? (expand)
    something that was a surprise? (unexpected)
    to tell how to do something or to give a reason for something? (explain)
    to want to do something very much? (desperately)
    to be worried or to care very much for something? (concerned)
    to feel much better about something? (relief)

5. Introduce the story. Have students look at the title page. Students should read the title and the description on the title page.

    What happened in the first book about Tidbit? This is the second in the series of three books that tells the story of Tidbit and his adventures.

    Students will begin reading *Tidbit to the Rescue*. The chapter numbers continue from the last Tidbit story, so the chapters are numbered from 5 to 8 in this book.

6. Use the handwriting sheet or have the children write the following sentences:

    The teacher explained how to solve the problem.
    I found an earthworm in the meadow.

LAR Answers

Part 1

1.	daydreamed	❍ short	● long
2.	breakfast	● short	❍ long
3.	weather	● short	❍ long
4.	season	❍ short	● long
5.	threads	● short	❍ long
6.	leader	❍ short	● long

Part 2

6	5
1	2
3	4
8	7

SAP Answers

Words can be in any order within each box

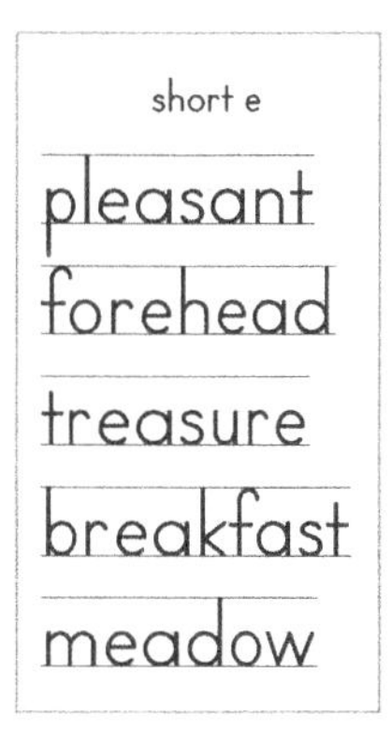

long e
teacher
season
meaning
increase
beagle

er search earthworm

long a steak

long u beautiful

Take the suffixes off these spelling words. Change the spelling of the root words if needed.

meaning mean

beautiful beauty

Lesson 57

Lesson Objectives

1. Students will review words spelled with ea. (P)
2. Students will nouns and verbs by context. (L)
3. Students will decode spelling words. (S)
4. Students will read the story *Tidbit to the Rescue*. (R)
5. Students will copy sentences neatly and correctly. (H)
6. Students will research and write about earthworms. (W)

Materials

LAR workbook page 59
SAP workbook page 50
WSW page 31
Book: *Tidbit to the Rescue*

Teaching

1. Write the words: head, earn, sea. Ask students the following questions:
   Look at these words. What do they have in common about the way they are spelled? (They all have the vowel digraph ea)

   What word means a place with a lot of water? (sea)
   What word means to make money? (earn)

   I have just said sentences that helped you choose the correct word. Now I'll ask you to make up a question that would help someone pick out this word. Point to the word head.

   The teacher should write a question based on the student responses. For example: What word is a part of the body?

   LAR part 1: **Read the words. Write questions that the words will answer.**

2. Ask students to give simple definitions for the term verb. (A verb is an action word. It tells what happens to the noun.) Ask students to name some verbs. Ask students for a definition of a noun. (person, place, or thing)

   Write the words run, ring, and staple. Ask students if the words are nouns or verbs. Students may say one or the other, but the correct answer is both. **These words could be nouns or they could be verbs. It will depend on their context in a sentence.**

   Read the following sentences. Say the underlined word first and ask students to listen to how it is used in the sentence. Is it a noun or verb?

   1. **We will <u>run</u> to the store.** (verb)
   2. **I scored the winning <u>run</u>.** (noun)
   3. **The <u>ring</u> had a large diamond.** (noun)
   4. **Did the telephone <u>ring</u>?** (verb)
   5. **The teacher will <u>staple</u> the papers.** (verb)
   6. **The <u>staple</u> stuck to the magnet.** (noun)

   The context determined whether the words were nouns or verbs. Some words are always verbs. Some words are always nouns, but there are some words that can be different parts of speech in different contexts. (Continued on the next page)

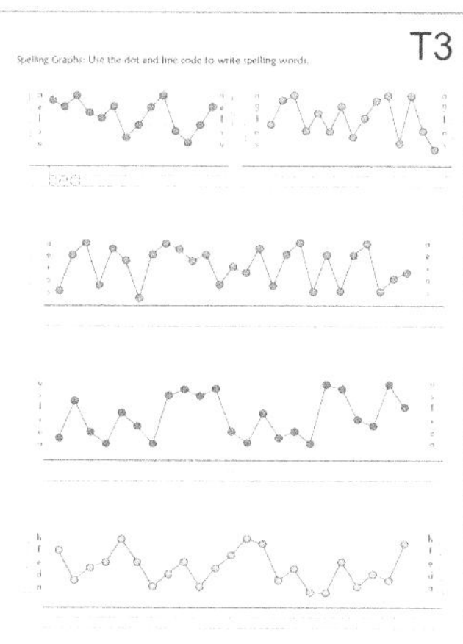

Part 2 of LAR workbook page 59: **Read the sentences. The underlined words are sometimes nouns and sometimes verbs. The sentence defines how they are used. Fill in the circle next to the words noun or verb to show how the underlined words are used in the sentences.**

3. Use the SAP workbook page. **You've probably seen graphs in math. In this exercise, your spelling words have been graphed. Use the dots to decode spelling words. Each line and space is assigned a letter. Look at the first set of lines. The first three letters are already written. See how the letters b-e-a match up to lines and spaces on the graph. More than one spelling word is written on each line. Decode the spelling words.**

4. Ask these questions about chapter five of *Tidbit to the Rescue* then begin reading chapter six.

   Why did Fritz tell Tidbit to always sniff the air? (to smell for cats)
   Why didn't Fritz follow Tidbit back to the nest? (He was too big to fit through the mouse hole.)
   How did the snake catch Tidbit? (by using its tongue)
   How did Tidbit save Fritz? (He poked the snake's mouth with a nail.)
   Why did tears form in Fritz's eyes at the end of the chapter? (Answers vary.)
   Have you ever been so happy that you've cried? Have you ever seen someone else that happy?

5. Use the handwriting sheet or have the children write the following sentences:

   Have you ever eaten steak for breakfast?
   The pirate desperately searched for the treasure.

6. Students will research to find three facts about earthworms. Students will use those facts in a story about searching for earthworms.

SAP Answers

Spelling Graphs: Use the dot and line code to write spelling words.

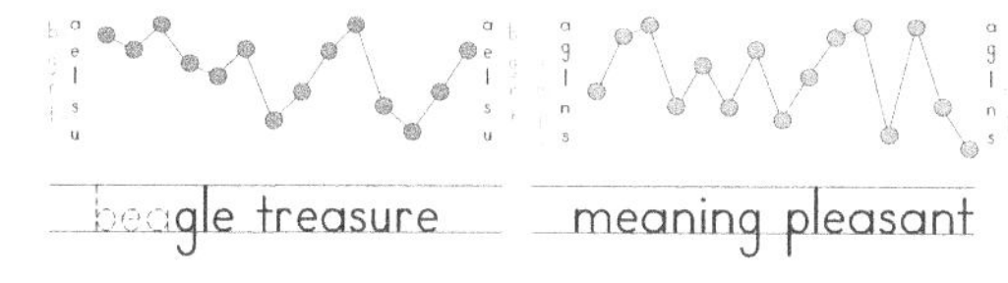

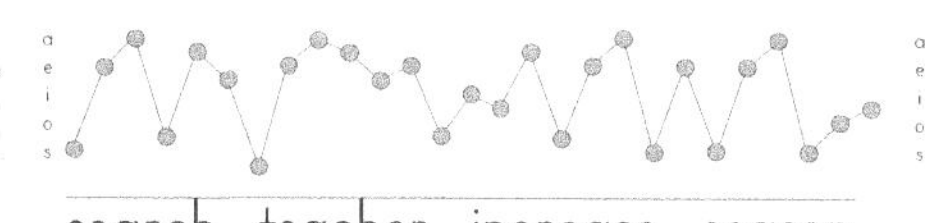

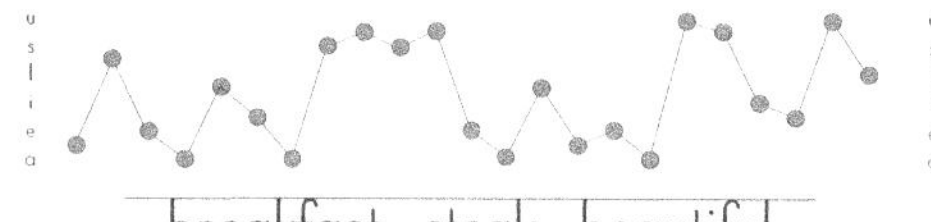

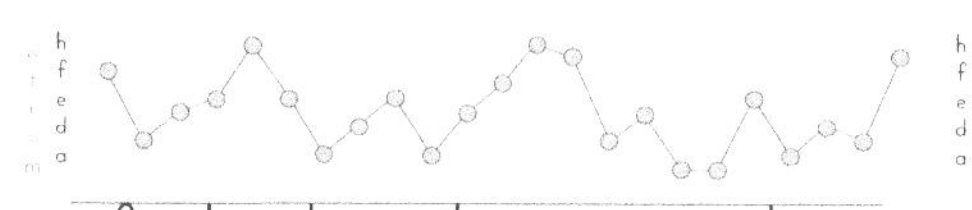

LAR Answers

Part 1

Answers vary.

Part 2

1. ❍ noun ● verb
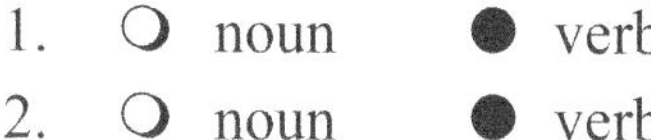
2. ❍ noun ● verb
3. ● noun ❍ verb
4. ● noun ❍ verb
5. ● noun ❍ verb
6. ● noun ❍ verb
7. ● noun ❍ verb
8. ❍ noun ● verb
9. ❍ noun ● verb
10. ❍ noun ● verb

Lesson 58

Lesson Objectives

1. Students will construct a paragraph. (L)
2. Students will review vocabulary words. (L)
3. Students will review the spelling list. (S)
4. Students will read part of the story *Tidbit to the Rescue*. (R)
5. Students will copy sentences neatly and correctly. (H)
6. Students will describe three different preferences. (W)

Materials

LAR workbook page 60
SAP workbook page 51
WSW page 32
Book: *Tidbit to the Rescue*

Teaching

1. Introduce the concept of a paragraph. **When we put the right combination of letters together we make a word. When we put the right combination of words together we make a sentence. What do we get when we put the right combination of sentences together?** Some students may answer a story. Explain that there is something with fewer sentences than a story. Introduce the term paragraph. Write the word *paragraph*.

   A paragraph is a group of sentences that work together to express an idea. Paragraphs usually have about four sentences. They can have more sentences, but usually not fewer than four.

   The first sentence usually tells the main idea of the paragraph. The next sentences tell or explain more about the main idea. The last sentence sums up the paragraph. For example:

   Baseball is a great sport. People love to watch it. Boys and girls can play baseball. Many people enjoy baseball games.

   What is the main idea? (Baseball is a great sport.)
   Why? (People love to watch it. Boys and girls can play baseball.)
   What sentence sums it up? (Many people enjoy baseball games.)

   You may also note that when paragraphs are written, the first word is usually indented, or moved over about the width of a five letter word.

   LAR workbook page 60: Have students read the paragraphs. Students will write the parts of the paragraph that answers the questions. Copy a sentence from the paragraph that answers the question.

2. Review the vocabulary words. Have students write sentences using the vocabulary words. You may dictate sentences or have students copy the following sentences about a picnic that was almost ruined by a storm:

   The *unexpected* dark clouds *concerned* us.
   We could not *explain* how they could *expand* so quickly.
   We *desperately* covered the picnic table.
   When the sun shined through it was a great *relief.*

   Discuss how the words were used in the sentences.

3. Use the SAP workbook page.

   Complete the sentences using the spelling words in the top box. One word will not be used. This is not the complete spelling list.

   Unscramble the spelling words and write them on the lines. Use the list in the green box.

4. Ask questions about chapter 6 of *Tidbit to the Rescue*, and then begin reading chapter 7.

   Describe Tidbit's nest. (The nest was made of torn paper, pillow stuffing, string, and yarn. It looked like a ball of fluff.)
   Why was Mrs. Mouse embarrassed when she talked to Fritz? (She thought most rats were awful.)
   Why did Fritz say rats and mice should get along? (They have the same enemies.)
   What did Fritz think happened to Tidbit's father? (He thought Mr. Mouse was captured.)
   Who do you think this enemy is? (Answers vary.)
   How do you think Fritz knows what happened to Mr. Mouse? (Answers vary.)

5. Use the handwriting sheet or have the children write the following sentences:

   It was a relief to find the beagle.
   The beautiful day was unexpected.

6. Students will describe their favorite season, breakfast, and treasure in a way that doesn't directly tell what it is. The reader should have enough clues to guess what it is. Have students think of the five senses. How would that time or thing feel, taste, look like (color, shape), sound, and feel. Describing winter for example: It feels wet when the snowflakes melt on my skin. The grass looks brown and the trees have no leaves.

LAR Answers

1. I hit the baseball as hard as I could.
2. The baseball sailed into the outfield.
3. Arnold tried to catch it.
4. I smiled all the way home.

5. Fall is a very nice season.
6. *Any or all of the following:* The leaves turn read and yellow. The weather is cool and pleasant. We feast on the fall harvest.
7. These are just a few reasons for loving the autumn season.

SAP Answers

earthworm forehead breakfast beautiful steak search meadow beagle

Did the lion eat a steak for breakfast?

I will search for an earthworm in the meadow.

The beagle has a brown spot on its forehead.

Unscramble the spelling words and write them on the lines.

teacher earthworm season pleasant meaning forehead treasure breakfast increase beautiful steak search meadow beagle

1. sanose season
2. arenuste treasure
3. gameinn meaning
4. cehcart teacher
5. secarien increase
6. staplena pleasant
7. flutiubac beautiful
8. domewa meadow

Lesson 59

Lesson Objectives

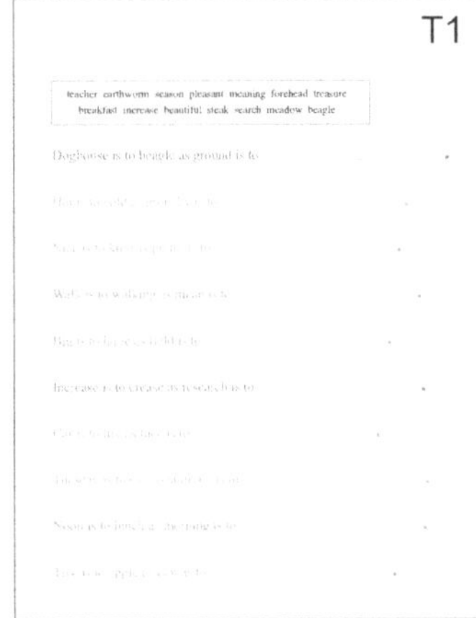

1. Students will review spelling words. (S)
2. Students will read the story *Tidbit to the Rescue.* (R)
3. Students will write a story. (CW)
4. Students will copy sentences neatly and correctly. (H)

Materials

SAP workbook page 52
Book: *Tidbit to the Rescue*

Teaching

1. Use the SAP workbook page. **Complete the analogies using spelling words.**

2. Ask questions about chapter 7.

   Why did Fritz believe a human had captured Tidbit's father? (There was a footprint outside the church. Tidbit's father's bag was next to it.)
   How did Tidbit almost drown? (He fell in the bucket of water.)
   What's a downspout? (It carries the rain water that falls on the roof from the gutters to the ground.)
   What do you think Tidbit felt about being rescued by a bird? (Answers vary.)
   What do you think Tidbit's father was feeling? (Answers vary.)
   How do you think Fritz will use the strange basket to save Timothy Mouse? (Answers vary.)
   How do you think the mice feel about being pets? (Answers vary.)

   Students will now read chapter 8 of the book *Tidbit to the Rescue.*

3. **Fritz had a strange flying machine. It helped him travel somewhere he couldn't go without it. What kind of machine could you make to go somewhere new? Would it be a balloon like Fritz's. Where would you go? What would you see? How would you get back? What problems might you have? How would you solve those problems? Write a story about your adventure in your special machine.**

4. Use the handwriting sheet or have the children write the following sentences:

   Spring is my favorite season.
   The weather is very pleasant.

SAP Answers

teacher earthworm season pleasant meaning forehead treasure
breakfast increase beautiful steak search meadow beagle

Doghouse is to beagle as ground is to earthworm.

Hot is to cold as grouchy is to pleasant.

Nice is to kind as pretty is to beautiful.

Walk is to walking as mean is to meaning.

Big is to large as field is to meadow.

Increase is to crease as research is to search.

Car is to tire as face is to forehead.

Tuesday is to day as summer is to season.

Noon is to lunch as morning is to breakfast.

Tree is to apple as cow is to steak.

Lesson 60

Lesson Objectives

1. Students will answer questions about the story *Tidbit to the Rescue*. (L)
2. Students will categorize words. (L)
3. Students will take a spelling test. (S)
4. Students will read the stories they have written. (R)
5. Students will copy a sentence neatly and correctly. (H)
6. Students will read and respond to a fable. (R)

Materials

Creative writing assignment
Book: *Tidbit to the Rescue*
LAR workbook pages 61
Resource Pack Fable Sheet

Teaching

1. Use part 1 of LAR workbook page 61. Answer the questions about the story.

2. Write the words, red, blue, green. **How are these three words alike?** (They're all colors.) **How are the words beak, feather, and wing alike?** (They are parts of birds.)

   Use part 2 of LAR workbook page 61. **Write sentences that tell how each group of words is alike.**

3. Have students number their paper from 1 to 14. Give the following words as dictation.

   1. treasure, 2. increase, 3. beagle, 4. breakfast, 5. season, 6. steak, 7. beautiful, 8. forehead, 9. teacher, 10. meaning, 11. earthworm, 12. pleasant, 13. search, 14. meadow

4. Have students read stories from the lesson 59 creative writing assignment.

5. Use the handwriting sheet or have the children write the following sentences:

   A crease was in my forehead.
   Expand and increase can have the same meaning.

6. Use the Fable Sheet. Students will read the fable *The Donkey and Her Driver*. Students will then write a story that could have the same moral. They will write about a character that refused to take good advice.

LAR Answers

Part 1

Answers will vary.
Suggested answers:

1. He poked it with a nail.
2. He saw a footprint.
3. A burning ember set it on fire.

Part 2

Answers will vary.
Suggested answers:

1. These are things you eat.
2. These are the four seasons of the year.
3. These are different kinds of weather.
4. All these are full of water.
5. These are parts of a tree.

Lesson 61

Lesson Objectives

1. Students will review the vowel digraph oa and diphthongs oi, oy. (P)
2. Students will spell words correctly. (S)
3. Students will learn the prefix pre-. (L)
4. Students will learn vocabulary words. (L)
5. Students will begin reading the story *Fritz and the Fire.* (R)
6. Students will copy sentences neatly and correctly. (H)

Materials

Dictionary
LAR workbook page 62
SAP workbook page 53
Book: *Fritz and the Fire*

Teaching

1. Write the words boil, toy, and coat. **What vowel do all of these words have in common?** (o) **In each of these words, o is used with another letter to make the vowel sound. What letters does o work with in the first two words to make the vowel sound?** (oi and oy) **Do they make the same sound?** (yes)

   Is it the same sound that you hear in the third word? (no) **What sound do you hear in that word?** (long o) **How is the long o sound spelled**? (oa)

2. Use the SAP workbook page. **Look at the spelling words in the box. They have either o-a, o-i, or o-y.** Go through each words in the list and have students identify which or the three digraphs is in the words.

   Alphabetize the words. The list is divided into two groups. On the bottom of the workbook page add suffixes to different words made from the root word *joy.* Don't forget to apply spelling rules for adding suffixes.

3. Write the words view and cook. Introduce the prefix, pre-. Write pre. **When we add the prefix p-r-e to the beginning of a word it changes the meaning. The prefix p-r-e means before. In fact, the word prefix has the prefix p-r-e on it.**

   A prefix is put before the beginning of a word. So *prefix* means fixed or attached to the beginning of a word. Look at the words *view* and *cook.* Add p-r-e. What are the new words? (preview, precook) Discuss the meanings of the words with the students. Have students say them in sentences.

   Preview *to see part of something before watching the whole thing*

   Precook *to partially cook something before final cooking*

   Use LAR workbook page 62. **The pictures illustrate two more words with the prefix p-r-e. Read the page. It includes a word list. Match the words to the definitions and complete the definitions using the root words of the words in the list.**

   Look at the example. The word *precancel* was written in the box and the word *cancel* was written on the line to complete the definition. *Precancel* means to cancel a postage stamp before mailing.

4. Introduce the vocabulary words for the story *Fritz and the Fire*. Students may look at the list on the back of the book.

confident, dangerous, hospitality, instructed, suspected, innocent

Ask the students which word fits the definitions:

Which word means:
not safe? (dangerous)
not guilty? (innocent)
to think something or someone caused a problem? (suspected)
to feel you can do something difficult? (confident)
to be taught something? (instructed)
to show kindness to a guest? (hospitality)

5. Introduce the story. Have students look at the title page. Students should read the title and the description on the title page.

Ask students to retell what happened in the story of Tidbit so far. This is the third in the series of three books that tell the story of Tidbit and his adventures.

Students will begin reading *Fritz and the Fire*. The chapter numbers continue from the last Tidbit story, so the chapters are numbered from 9 to 12 in this book.

6. Use the handwriting sheet or have the children write the following sentences:

It is dangerous to approach the dam in a rowboat.
The cowboy was employed at the ranch.

LAR Answers

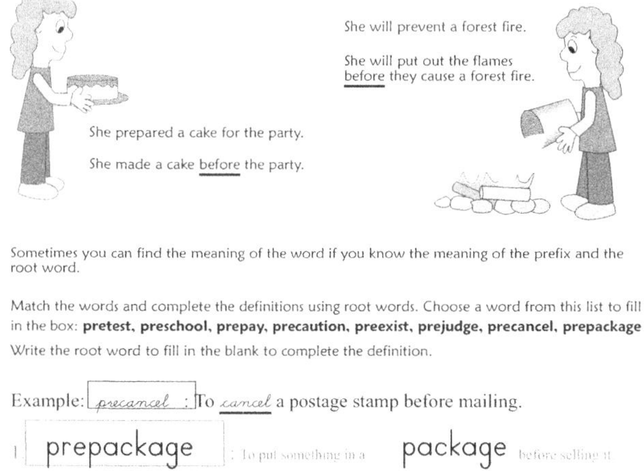

SAP Answers

Lesson 62

Lesson Objectives

1. Students will review capitalization. (L)
2. Students will identify the subject part of a sentence. (L)
3. Students will divide spelling words into syllables. (S)
4. Students will read the story *Fritz and the Fire*. (R)
5. Students will copy sentences neatly and correctly. (H)
6. Students will research and then write facts and opinions. (W)

Materials

LAR workbook page 63
SAP workbook page 54
WSW page 33
Book: *Fritz and the Fire*

Teaching

1. Use the top of LAR workbook page 63 to review capitalization rules. **Proper nouns are names of people, places, or things. Look at the top of the workbook page for examples. What are some other proper nouns? Proper nouns are always capitalized.**

   Look at the sentences. Underline the words that need to be capitalized.

2. **Sentences have different parts. The part that tells who or what the sentence is about is called the subject part of the sentence. The part that tells what it does is called the predicate part of the sentence. Today we will find the subject parts of sentences.** Read this sentence: **The furry little kitten drank the cream.**

   What is this sentence about? (The furry little kitten) **This is the subject part of the sentence.**

   Repeat for the following two sentences (the subject part is underlined). Write at least one where students can see it. Underline the subject part after students respond:

   <u>The loud siren</u> came from the fire truck.
   <u>The blue computer</u> is new.

   Use the bottom of LAR workbook page 63. Read the sentences. Underline the subject part of each sentence.

3. Review dividing words into syllables. Use the SAP workbook page. **Syllables are parts of words. Every syllable has one vowel sound. Syllables can have more than one vowel as long as the vowels work together to make only one sound. Look at the workbook page.**

   There are other rules for dividing words. Each color is a new rule. Read the rules and divide the spelling words that are listed using that rule. The rules are reprinted from the workbook page below:

   Compound words are divided between the two words. Divide these two words: toadstool, rowboat.

   Prefixes or suffixes usually form their own syllable. Divide these three words: toaster, rejoice, avoid.

When vowels form a digraph like oi, ea, oy, and ai, do not divide between those vowels. The words are usually divided right after vowel digraphs if

they're followed by a vowel, consonant digraph, or single consonant. Divide these three words: loyal, voyage, poison.

When two or more consonants come between vowels, the words are usually divided between the two consonants. Divide these six words: porpoise, sirloin, employ, moisture, approach, oyster

4. Ask these questions about chapter 9 of *Fritz and the Fire* then begin reading chapter 10.

   Did Fritz know what happened to Tidbit? (no) **How do you know this?** (Answers vary.)
   Where is Tidbit? (in the bucket)
   What happened to the balloon? (It hit a tree.)
   Where did the rat stay? (Fritz stayed in an owl's nest.)
   Why was this bad place for Fritz to be? (Owls eat mice and rats.)
   Fritz made a plan to keep safe from the owl. We don't know what it is yet. What do you think his plan will be? (Answers vary.)

5. Use the handwriting sheet or have the children write the following sentences:

   The moisture helped the toadstool grow.
   Can the porpoise eat an oyster?

6. Students will research and write two facts about porpoises and oysters. Students will also write an opinion about porpoises and oysters.

LAR Answers

Underline the letters that need to be capitalized.

1. Does roy live on boyd road?
2. Is boise the capital of idaho?
3. Did joyce buy the new toyota?
4. Has troy ever been to oakland, california?
5. Did you see joan in des moines, iowa?

Read the of sentences. Underline the subject parts.

Example:

The tiny blue rowboat was filled with oysters

1. Our new sleeping bags were moisture proof.
2. The blue sailboat left on a dangerous voyage.
3. The king employed servants to show hospitality.
4. The rough and tough cowboy liked sirloin steaks.
5. The yellow toaster oven cooked the tiny pizzas.

SAP Answers

Divide the words into syllables.

Rule 1: All syllables must have a vowel sound.

cow/boy

toad stool row boat

a bout de crease walk ing

toast er re joice a void

roy al may or

loy al voy age poi son

ap ply tor toise

por poise sir loin em ploy

mois ture ap proach oys ter

Lesson 63

Lesson Objectives

1. Students will complete sentences in context of a paragraph (cloze). (L)
2. Students will review vocabulary words. (L)
3. Students will review the spelling list. (S)
4. Students will read part of the story *Fritz and the Fire.* (R)
5. Students will copy sentences neatly and correctly. (H)
6. Students will write descriptions of books. (W)

Materials

LAR workbook page 64
SAP workbook page 55
WSW page 34
Book: *Fritz and the Fire*

Teaching

1. The following exercise is a cloze exercise. Students are presented with sentences that are not complete. The best word to complete the sentences not only relies on the sentence context, but also the context of the paragraph: therefore, students have to link the ideas within the sentences together to get the correct answers.

   Read the following paragraph one sentence at a time. Stop after each sentence and have students make a prediction as to the correct answer.

   Read the first sentence and ask students for possible words to complete the sentence. Write the words where students can see them. Then read the next sentence. Ask the students which guesses for the first sentence still work or should a different word be used. Discuss how hearing the second sentence helped decide the best answer for the first sentence. Continue through the paragraph in the same manner. **This is why it is important to read all the sentences before filling in any words.**

   The most probable answers are in parentheses, but other answers might work.

   We enjoy spending the day at the _____. (beach) **We stand on it and watch the huge ocean waves. Our family loves to _____ in the sand.** (dig, play) **We each have little shovels to do this. Sometimes we find ____ in the sand.** (money, coins, things) **I found a silver quarter once. The _______ is a great place to find things.** (beach, sand)

   Part 1 of LAR workbook page 64: Have students read the paragraph with missing words. Students will choose the word that best completes the sentences. Students should read the whole paragraph before choosing answers.

2. Review the vocabulary words. Use the bottom part of the LAR workbook page. **Look at the vocabulary words in the box. What does each word mean?**

   Word list: confident, dangerous, hospitality, instructed, suspected, innocent. **Complete the sentences on the bottom of the page using the vocabulary words.**

3. Use SAP workbook page 55. Students will use spelling words to fill in the letters in the boxes. Start with the boxes with clues (letters). Cross words off the list as they are written.

4. Ask questions about chapter 10 of *Fritz and the Fire*. Then begin reading chapter 11.

   How did the girl's mom trick her? (She asked what was in the bucket, when the girl was hiding it.)
   How many mice did Hannah think she had caught? (one)
   How did Tidbit's father feel about being caught? (calm) **Why?**
   If you were a mouse, would you like to be a pet or a wild mouse? Why?
   What do you think will happen next?
   Do you think Fritz will rescue them? Why or why not?

5. Use the handwriting sheet or have the children write the following sentences:

   Dad instructed me to avoid using the toaster.
   We rejoiced when the voyage began.

6. Based simply on a title, students will make up a description of a book with one of the titles. These aren't actual books in print (that we know of), so students can be creative with the descriptions. Students have the option of making up their own title as long as they use a spelling or vocabulary word in the title. You may have students look for examples of book descriptions either on webpages that sell books or book covers. The stories in the McRuffy reading books also have story descriptions on title pages.

LAR Answers

Part 1

The snake ________ (slithered, hid, coiled) through the brush. The little mouse was ________ (aware, afraid, unaware) of the danger it was in. It calmly nibbled on some ________ (snakes, seeds, eating) outside its cozy den. Just then the mouse heard the flutter of ______ (the snake, leaves, wings). A ____ (chicken, hawk, falcon) had swooped down onto the snake. The mouse _______ (watched, was caught, ate cheese) as the hawk flew away with a snake clutched in its talons. The hunter had become the prey.

Part 2

dangerous
instructed
hospitality
suspected
innocent
confident

SAP Answers

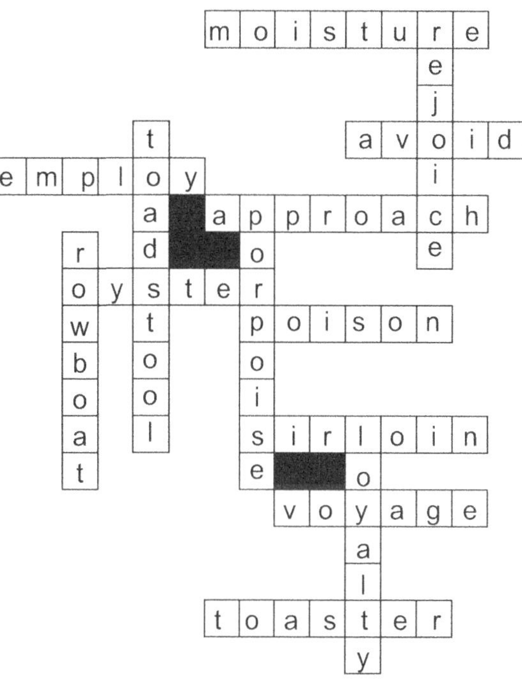

Lesson 64

Lesson Objectives

1. Students will review spelling words. (S)
2. Students will read the story *Fritz and the Fire.* (R)
3. Students will write a story. (CW)
4. Students will copy sentences neatly and correctly. (H)
5. Students will capitalize titles of books. (L)

Materials

SAP workbook page 56
Book: *Fritz and the Fire*
Resource Pack: Book title capitalization rules and lesson 64 practice sheet

Teaching

1. Use the SAP workbook page. **Write the spelling words that match the descriptions on the lines.**

2. Ask questions about chapter 11.

   Describe how the trap that Fritz made worked. (He used his balloon. When the owl landed on it, air was pushed into the tank. Hot embers flew out of the tank and hit the owl.)
   What is the problem with hateful acts? (Innocent people get hurt.)
   What happened to the farmhouse? (It caught on fire.)
   According to the story, what is bravery? (Doing something to help others, even when you're afraid.)
   How did the rat wake the people? (He rang a bell.)
   What should you do if you see a fire? (call 911, get an adult, etc.)
   Is it a good idea for you to run into a burning building? (No) **Why not?**

   Students will now read chapter 12 of the book *Tidbit to the Rescue.*

3. **Tidbit became a pet. There are probably good things about being a pet and bad things about being a pet. What do you think those things would be? If you were a pet, what kind of pet would you be? What would you like or not like about it? Or, if you have a pet, what do you think it likes and dislikes about being a pet. Write about it!**

4. Use the handwriting sheet or have the children write the following sentences:

   The neighbor suspected that our dog ate the sirloin.
   We were confident that our dog was innocent.

5. Use the book title capitalization sheet as rules for capitalizing book titles are introduced. These are the rules for capitalizing titles of books, magazines, poems, movies, newspapers, stories, paintings, and other artistic works.

   Less significant words are only capitalized if they are the first or last word of a title:

   articles: a, an, the
   prepositions less than 5 letters such as: in, on, of, to
   conjunctions less than 5 letters such as: and, but, or, for
   A word after a colon in a title is capitalized. The Bobcat Cowboys: A Cat Tale

Other short words are capitalized, for example:
Verbs: was, are, were, be.
Pronouns: my, he, his, she

Have students capitalize the titles on the lesson 64 book title capitalization practice sheet.

These are titles of actual books. McRuffy Press has not reviewed all the books and although the list may contain many quality books, McRuffy Press is not necessarily endorsing them.

Practice Sheet Answers

My Side of the Mountain
Bridge to Terabithia
The Watsons Go to Birmingham
Island of the Blue Dolphins
The Sign of the Beaver
Mrs. Frisby and the Rats of Nimh
I Am the Ice Worm
Baseball in April and Other Stories

SAP Answers

toaster loyalty sirloin voyage
approach oyster rowboat rejoice
toadstool moisture porpoise
employ avoid poison

A kind of steak
sirloin

employ

To go near
approach

Makes things damp
moisture

Like a mushroom
toadstool

It has a shell
oyster

Use it to heat breakfast.
toaster

It's like a dolphin.
porpoise

To stay with someone
loyalty

Ride it in the water
rowboat

Stay away
avoid

Be happy
rejoice

It can make you sick.
poison

voyage

Lesson 65

Lesson Objectives

1. Students will answer questions about the story *Fritz and the Fire.* (L)
2. Students will add details to sentences. (L)
3. Students will take a spelling test. (S)
4. Students will read the stories they have written. (R)
5. Students will copy a sentence neatly and correctly. (H)

Materials

LAR workbook pages 65
Creative writing assignment
Book: *Fritz and the Fire*

Teaching

1. Use part 1 of LAR workbook page 65. Answer the questions about the story.

2. Write the sentence: The dog barked. Have students read it. **This sentence doesn't tell us very much. There are no details in this sentence. If you were writing this sentence in a story, you could make it much better by adding some details.**

   Write the words, who, what, where, when, and why. **Think of the sentence: The dog barked. Look at these words that begin with W. These words are often used to ask questions. These are often called the 5 W's.**

   We can add details to the sentence to answer these questions. For example, who barked? Let's add details that tell more about the dog.

   Fred's dog barked. Now we know more about who the dog is. What was the dog barking at? (Have students make suggestions and rewrite the sentence. For example, cat. Fred's dog barked at a cat.)

   Continue with the other three w's. The sentences do not need to keep building each time. You can start over with, The dog barked. Have students suggest questions and answers. For example:

   Where did the dog bark? The dog barked in the back yard.
   When did the dog bark? The dog barked all night long.
   Why did the dog bark? The angry dog barked.

   Use part two of LAR workbook page 65. Students read the simple sentences and add details that answer the 5 W questions.

3. Have students number their paper from 1 to 14. Give the following words as dictation.

   1. rowboat, 2. sirloin, 3. moisture, 4. approach, 5. porpoise, 6. rejoice, 7. poison, 8. loyalty, 9. avoid, 10. oyster, 11. toadstool, 12. toaster, 13. employ, 14. voyage

4. Have students read stories from the creative writing assignment.

5. Use the handwriting sheet or have the children write the following sentences:

   The old cowboy showed great hospitality.
   He also showed great loyalty to his employer.

LAR Answers

Part 1

Answers will vary.
Suggested answers:

1. It had lots of good things in it.
2. Fritz tricked it. It caught on fire.
3. Lightning started the fire.

Part 2

Answers will vary.

Lesson 66

Lesson Objectives

1. Students will review the vowel digraph ie and the vowel sounds of y. (P)
2. Students will spell words correctly. (S)
3. Students will categorize words. (L)
4. Students will learn vocabulary words. (L)
5. Students will begin reading the story *Bobcat Cowboys On Trial*. (R)
6. Students will copy sentences neatly and correctly. (H)

Materials

Dictionary
LAR workbook page 66
SAP workbook page 57
Book: *Bobcat Cowboys On Trial*

Teaching

1. Write the words field and tie. **What vowels do these two words have in common?** (ie) **Do they make the same sound?** (no) **What vowel sound do you hear in the word field?** (long e) **What vowel sound do you hear in the word tie?** (long i)

   Write the words try and hurry. **What is the last letter in these two words?** (y) **Do they make the same sound?** (no) **What sound does Y make in the word try?** (long i) **What sound does Y make in the word hurry?** (long e)

   When we add suffixes that begin with e such as e-d or e-s to words that end in with Y what happens to the Y? (Drop the y and add i) Change try to tries and hurry to hurried. Have students read the words. **Does the i-e in the suffixes make the same sound as the Y did before it was dropped?** (yes)

2. Use the SAP workbook page. **Look at the workbook page. These words have either i-e or y in them making the long e or long i sounds.** Go through the list. Have students find the y or i-e. Ask students to identify the long vowel sound as either long e or long i.

   Spelling List: achieve, magnify, pies, motorcycle, ability, believe, multiplied, windshield, everything, butterflies, why, movies, shriek, country

   Alphabetize the spelling words in each box. At the bottom of the workbook page, write the singular form of the three words. Change the spelling of the root word if needed. (butterfly)

3. Write the words chalk, pencil, and pen. **How are these words alike?** (They are things used for drawing or writing.) **Now let's do something different. This time I will say how things are alike and you tell me three words. These are kinds of pets.** (Students should respond by saying three types of pets such as dog, cat, and bird.)

   Use LAR workbook page 66 part 1. Have students read the sentences that describe categories. Students will write three words to fit each category.

   Ask students to write some of their own categories on a blank piece of paper. Student should come up with three things that fit the category. Ask other students to come up with more things that fit the category.

4. Introduce the vocabulary words for the story *Bobcat Cowboys On Trial.* Students may look at the list on the title page of the book.

   hippopotamus, porcupine, prosecuting, stenotype

   Make sure students can read the words. Students should know the meanings of the animal words.

   The word stenotype is defined in the context of the story and on the LAR workbook page. Help students derive the meaning of prosecuting from the glossary (prosecuting attorney).

   Students should also read through the words listed in the Courtroom Glossary on page 1. Students may refer back to the glossary during the story.

5. Introduce the story. Have students look at the title page. Students should read the title and the description on the title page.

   Students continuing from the Second Grade curriculum may remember other stories involving the Bobcat Cowboys. Ask students what a trial is. Tell students that they will begin reading about the trial of the Bobcat Cowboys. Ask students to make guesses as to what the Bobcats did wrong.

   Students will begin reading *Bobcat Cowboys On Trial.* The book is presented in three parts over the next three weeks. Part 1 contains Chapters 1 to 4. Have students begin reading Chapter 1.

6. Use the handwriting sheet or have the children write the following sentences:

   The butterflies landed on the hippopotamus.
   The broken windshield is dangerous.

LAR Answers

Answers vary.

SAP Answers

Word List
achieve
magnify
pies
motorcycle
ability
believe
multiplied
windshield
everything
butterflies
why
movies
shriek
country

Alphabetize each set of words.

country butterflies
everything achieve
pies ability believe

1 ability
2 achieve
3 believe
4 butterflies
5 country
6 everything
7 pies

windshield magnify
why movies shriek
multiplied motorcycle

1 magnify
2 motorcycle
3 movies
4 multiplied
5 shriek
6 why
7 windshield

Change the word to mean one. Write the singular form of each word.

butterflies butterfly

pies pie

movies movie

Lesson 67

Lesson Objectives

1. Students will review the vowel digraph ie the long vowel sounds of y. (P)
2. Students will identify the predicate part of a sentence. (L)
3. Students will identify the vowel digraph ie the long vowel sounds of y. (P)
4. Students will read part of the story *Bobcat Cowboys On Trial*. (R)
5. Students will copy sentences neatly and correctly. (H)
6. Students will write opinions and facts about animales. (W)

Materials

LAR workbook page 67
SAP workbook page 58
WSW page 35
Book: *Bobcat Cowboys On Trial*

Teaching

1. Use LAR workbook page 67: Solve the crossword puzzle using words with y and ie. A word list is provided.

2. **We learned last week that sentences have different parts. The part that tells who or what the sentence is about is called the subject part of the sentence. The part that tells what it does is called the predicate part of the sentence.**

   Today we will find the predicate parts of sentences. Read this sentence: **The big gorilla threw a banana.**

   What is the subject part of the sentence? (The big gorilla) **The rest of the sentence tells what the big gorilla did. What did the gorilla do?** (threw a banana)

   This is called the predicate part of the sentence. The predicate part of the sentence tells what the subject does. I'm going to underline the predicate part of the sentence. Underline *threw a banana.*

   Repeat for the following two sentences (the predicate part is underlined). Write the sentences. Underline the predicate part after students identify it:

   The loud siren <u>came from the fire truck</u>.
   The blue computer <u>is new</u>.

   Write a third sentence that students dictate to you. Have students identify the predicate.

   Ask students to write more sentences on blank paper. Students should underline the predicate parts.

3. Use the SAP workbook page. **Look at the workbook page. There are fourteen sentences with the spelling words underlined. Does the underlined word have a long e or long i sound? Fill in the circles to mark your answers.**

4. Ask the questions about chapter 1 of *Bobcat Cowboys On Trial* then begin reading chapter 2.

   Describe Sheriff Prairie Dog's gun. (a gun that shoots rubber bands that are held on with a clothespin)
   What happened when Papa Prairie Dog tested the gun? (The rubber band went off. It hit the lantern and Miss Fussybunny.)
   What lesson about guns can be learned from this? (Never assume a gun won't go off. Be careful.)
   What happened to Otto Muskrat? (He sat in a hole in the bench and got stuck.)
   Why didn't he want Tumbly to help him? (He didn't like getting stuck by the porcupine's quills.)
   Why was everyone afraid of Judge Polecat? (He was known as the "hangin' judge.")
   What do you think will happen next in the story?

5. Use the handwriting sheet or have the children write the following sentences:

   You can achieve more if you believe.
   The magnifying glass multiplied the size.

6. Students will research and write two facts about a hippopotamus and a porcupine. Students will also write an opinion about each.

LAR Answers

								3 F	R	I	E	N	D	4 L	Y
1 D	R	I	E	2 D										I	
R				R				7 H			8 S			E	
A				I			6 F	A	M	I	L	I	11 E	S	
5 G	R	I	Z	Z	L	Y		P			O		V		
O				Z				10 P	U	P	P	I	E	S	
N			9 S	L	E	E	P	Y			P		R		
12 F	I	F	T	Y					13 F	L	Y		Y		
L			O						R				T		
Y		14 C	R	Y				15 M	Y			19 S	H	Y	
			I					A					I		
	16 P	I	E	17 S				N					N		
			18 S	L	U	S	H	Y			20 A	N	G	R	Y
				Y											

SAP Answers

1. ○ Long e ● Long i
2. ○ Long e ● Long i
3. ● Long e ○ Long i
4. ● Long e ○ Long i
5. ○ Long e ● Long i
6. ○ Long e ● Long i
7. ● Long e ○ Long i
8. ○ Long e ● Long i
9. ○ Long e ● Long i
10. ● Long e ○ Long i
11. ● Long e ○ Long i
12. ● Long e ○ Long i
13. ● Long e ○ Long i
14. ● Long e ○ Long i

Lesson 68

Lesson Objectives

1. Students will explain similes. (L)
2. Students will review vocabulary words. (L)
3. Students will review the spelling list. (S)
4. Students will read part of the story *Bobcat Cowboys On Trial.* (R)
5. Students will copy sentences neatly and correctly. (H)
6. Students will map a chain of events. (W)

Materials

LAR workbook page 68
SAP workbook page 59
WSW page 36
Book: *Bobcat Cowboys On Trial*

Teaching

1. **A simile is a figure of speech where two essentially unlike things are compared. But, they are alike in some way that we don't normally think about. So, this makes us think more about the special way the two things are alike. A simile often uses the words as or like to compare the two things.**

   Here is an example of a simile: I'm as hungry as an elephant. An elephant is a very big animal that eats a lot. So, saying *I'm as hungry as an elephant* is an interesting way to say I'm very hungry.

   What do you think this one means? My horse is as old as the hills. (The horse is very old.) **Why?** The hills have to be older than anything on them.

   LAR workbook page 68: Students will write a sentence telling what each simile means.

2. Have students review the words in the glossary. Ask students to identify the characters that match the definitions of bailiff (mouse), defendant (Bobcat Cowboys), defense attorney (Frazzle O'Hare), prosecuting attorney (Alice McHoot), and the jury (weasels, foxes, wolves, coyotes, rat).

   Discuss the meanings of the words.

3. Use the SAP workbook page. **Look at the spelling words at the top of the page. They are written with lots of space between the letters. The words aren't spelled correctly. Letters are missing. Write the missing letters where they belong. Some words may need more than one letter.**

   At the bottom of the workbook page are short words with lines after them. Look for the letters for the short words in the spelling word list. The spelling words are numbered. If you can make the short word with the letters of the spelling word, write the spelling word's number on the line. Find numbers for each line.

4. Ask questions about chapter 2 of *Bobcat Cowboys On Trial*, then begin reading chapter 3.

   Why did the animals think the mouse was pretending to be a horse? (Because the word horse sounds like the word hoarse.)
   What does it mean to have a frog in your throat? (It means that it is hard to talk, usually because of a sore throat.)
   Why were the critters afraid of Alice McHoot? (Because owls eat small animals.)
   What was her dream? (to be an attorney for farm animals)
   Why was Frazzle O'Hare afraid of the jury? (They looked like they wanted to eat him.)
   How did the judge help Frazzle? (He asked the sheriff to get the jury and Alice some hamburgers.)
   Why? (To make them less hungry.)
   What do you think will happen next?

5. Use the handwriting sheet or have the children write the following sentences:

   Why did that colorful bird shriek?
   We rode a motorcycle to the country.

6. Students will write the chain of events in Chapter 1 of *The Bobcat Cowboys on Trial.* Students will make a summary of each step from Sheriff Prairie Dog hugging his father to Sheriff Prairie Dog putting out a fire. The events are on pages 159 to 160 of Reading Book 1. Students should use transition words (see page 2 of the Writing Skills Workbook).

SAP Answers

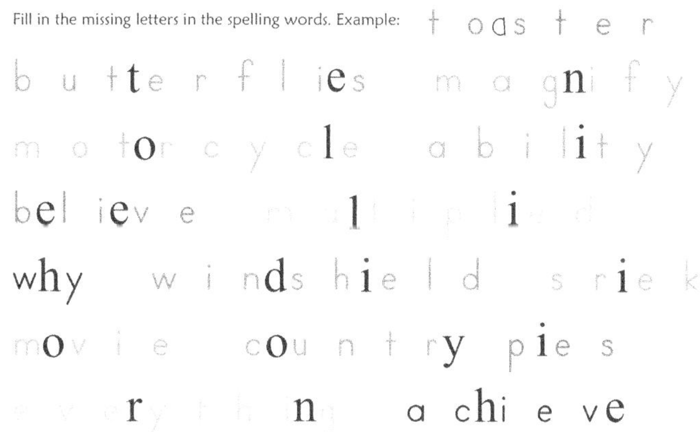

1. achieve
2. magnify
3. pies
4. motorcycle
5. ability
6. believe
7. multiplied
8. windshield
9. everything
10. butterflies
11. why
12. movies
13. shriek
14. country

What spelling words can make the small words. Write their numbers on the lines.

he 1,8,9,13 bee 6, 10
is 3,8,10,12,13 5,7,9,10
or 4,14 I'm 2,7,12 eve 1,6,9
4,9,14 let 4,7,10 10,14
bat 5 in 2,8,9

LAR Answers

Answer vary
Sample answers

1. Trish felt like she didn't belong.
2. We'll be there very soon.
3. The truck was very slow.
4. My throat is very dry.
5. The boy is a good swimmer.

Lesson 69

Lesson Objectives

1. Students will review spelling words. (S)
2. Students will read part of the story *Bobcat Cowboys On Trial.* (R)
3. Students will write a story. (CW)
4. Students will copy sentences neatly and correctly. (H)
5. Students will capitalize titles of books. (L)

Materials

SAP workbook page 60
Book: *Bobcat Cowboys On Trial*
Resource Pack: Book title capitalization rules and lesson 69 practice sheet

Teaching

1. Have students sort and write the spelling words into four groups. Words where ie makes the long e sound, words where ie makes the long i sound, words where y makes the long e sound, words where y makes the long i sound.

   Answers: Long e spelled ie: achieve, believe, windshield, shriek, movies
   Long i spelled ie: butterflies, pies, multiplied
   Long e spelled y: everything, country, ability
   Long i spelled y: motorcycle, , magnify, why

   SAP workbook: **Write spelling words to match the descriptions.**

2. Ask questions about chapter 3.

   Who are the defendants in the trial? (Billybob, Bobbybill, and Bubba)
   What is a stenograph machine? (a machine that the court reporter uses to type in the words said in a trail)
   Why do you think it would be important to type all the words said in a trial? (Answers vary.)
   What was Alice McHoot's favorite food? (carrots)
   What did the other animals think she wanted to eat? (them)
   How do you know that? (They all ran when she asked them to lunch.)
   What did the wolf do that was wrong? (It ate the rat.)
   What did the wolf mean when he said the rat would rat on him? (tell on him)
   What do you think will happen next?

   Students will now read chapter 4 of the book *Bobcat Cowboys On Trial.*

3. **Now the wolf is in jail for eating the rat. What do you think will happen at the wolf's trial? What will the rat say? How do you think the wolf will be punished? Write a story telling what happened at the wolf's trial.**

   Alternative assignment: Write a short report about a porcupine or hippopotamus.

4. Use the handwriting sheet or have the children write the following sentences:

   The same prosecuting attorney was in two movies.
   The judges liked mom's apple pies.

5. Use the book title capitalization sheet as rules for capitalizing book titles are introduced. These are the rules for capitalizing titles of books, magazines, poems, movies, newspapers, stories, paintings, and other artistic works. Following is a review of the rules.

   Less significant words are only capitalized if they are the first or last word of a title:

   articles: a, an, the
   prepositions less than 5 letters such as: in, on, of, to
   conjunctions less than 5 letters such as: and, but, or, for
   A word after a colon in a title is capitalized. The Bobcat Cowboys: A Cat Tale

   Other short words are capitalized, for example:
   Verbs: was, are, were, be.
   Pronouns: my, he, his, she

   Have students capitalize the titles on the lesson 69 book title capitalization practice sheet.

   These are titles of actual books. McRuffy Press has not reviewed all the books and although the list may contain many quality books, McRuffy Press is not necessarily endorsing them.

Practice Sheet Answers

The Pepins and Their Problems
Roll of Thunder Hear My Cry
Little House on the Prairie
The Last of the Mohicans
James and the Giant Peach
The Indian in the Cupboard
The Wheel on the School
Lad: A Dog

SAP Answers

Use the clues to find the spelling words. A list is in the orange box.

achieve magnify pies motorcycle ability
believe multiplied windshield everything
butterflies why movies shriek country

United States of America
country

To make something look larger
magnify

It has two wheels.
motorcycle

Opposite of nothing
everything

To do good things
achieve

They have wings.
butterflies

A part of a car
windshield

Apple, cream, peach, pumpkin
pies

Six times seven
multiplied

You can do it if you have this.
ability

A loud, shrill, sound
shriek

The reason
why

Tell stories with pictures.
movies

believe

Lesson 70

Lesson Objectives

1. Students will answer questions about the story *Bobcat Cowboys On Trial.* (L)
2. Students will answer questions requiring inference. (L)
3. Students will take a spelling test. (S)
4. Students will read the stories they have written. (R)
5. Students will copy a sentence neatly and correctly. (H)
6. Students will read and respond to fables. (R)

Materials

Creative writing assignment
Book: *Bobcat Cowboys On Trial*
LAR workbook pages 69
Resource Pack Fable Sheet

Teaching

1. Use the top section of LAR workbook page 69. Answer the questions about the story.

2. **Sometimes when we read our stories in reading, you are asked questions. Some questions just ask you to remember something about what you've read. But there are different kinds of questions.**

   Sometimes you need to answer a question using information you already knew before the story and combine that with information in the story. The story may not tell you the exact answer. You kind of have to guess. This guess based on what you already know is called inference.

   I'll read a little story for example: Christy put on her heavy coat. She wrapped her favorite scarf around her neck. The scarf reminded her of the bright sun. She wouldn't be seeing the sun today. She opened the door and felt the chilly breeze.

   What time of year is it? (probably winter) **Why do you think so?** (Christy put on a coat, so it must be cold.) **The story doesn't tell us it is winter, but we can be pretty sure it is. The story infers that it is a cold time of the year and winter is cold. So we used inference to make a very good guess.**

   Discuss the other inference questions in the same way:

   What color was the scarf? (yellow, or orange – the color of the sun)
   Was it cloudy or sunny outside?
   Was Christy inside or outside when she put on her coat?

   Use part 2 of LAR workbook page 69. **Read the short story and answer the questions using inference.**

3. Have students number their paper from 1 to 14. Give the following words as dictation.

   1. butterflies, 2. pies, 3. believe, 4. country, 5. everything, 6. shriek, 7. multiplied, 8. motorcycle, 9. why, 10. ability, 11. windshield, 12. movies, 13. achieve, 14. magnify

4. Have students read stories from the lesson 69 creative writing assignment.

5. Use the handwriting sheet or have the children write the following sentences:

   A porcupine has the ability to throw quills.
   The court reporter typed on a stenograph machine.

6. Use the Fable Sheet. Students will read the fables *The Farmer and the Stork* and *The Two Goats*. Students will then compare the morals from both fables. Students will explain which lesson was most helpful and why.

LAR Answers

Wording of answers will vary on both parts.

Part 1

1. Miss Fussybunny fell on his tail.
2. The mouse couldn't talk.
3. He thought some animals were going to eat him.
4. A wolf ate it.
5. They thought the trial was on a road.

Part 2

1. for a birthday party
2. no
3. white
4. chocolate
5. a dog or puppy

Lesson 71

Lesson Objectives

1. Students will review consonant digraphs (sh, th, ch, wh, ph). (P)
2. Students will spell words correctly. (S)
3. Students will complete analogies. (L)
4. Students will learn vocabulary words. (L)
5. Students will begin reading the story *Bobcat Cowboys On Trial* part 2. (R)
6. Students will copy sentences neatly and correctly. (H)

Materials

Dictionary
LAR workbook page 70
SAP workbook page 61
Book: *Bobcat Cowboys On Trial* part 2

Teaching

1. Write the digraphs sh, th, ch, wh, and ph. **Most of the time each sound is written with one letter. Some sounds we write with two letters. These are called digraphs. Di- means the number two and graph means write.**

   Digraphs are sounds written with two letters. Can you think of words that have these digraphs in them? Let's start with *sh*. Have the students say words with the digraph *sh*. Write the words as students say them. Continue with the other digraphs.

2. Use the SAP workbook page. **Look at the words in the pink box. The words contain consonant digraphs. A consonant digraph is two letters that make a single sound. Look at the boxes with lines. What digraphs are in each box?** (ch, th, sh,. wh, ph) Have students read the words in the list and identify the digraph and its sound in each word.

   Sort the words by the digraph they contain. Write the words on the lines. On the bottom section make three compound words from the three mixed up compounds. Switched parts between the three words.

   Spelling List: orchard, shadow, together, sandwich, leather, whenever, theater, parachute, alphabet, sunshine, thanksgiving, whisper, shrub, paragraph, somewhere, Christmas

3. Use LAR workbook page 70. **Fill in the circles to complete each analogy.**

4. Introduce the vocabulary words for the story *Bobcat Cowboys On Trial* part 2. Students may look at the list on the back of the book.

   customer, disturbing, dreadful, opossum, panicking, serious

   Ask the students which word fits the definitions:

   Which word:
   Is a kind of animal? (opossum – considering the o as silent is an acceptable way to pronounce the word - possum)
   Means to change something or bother someone? (disturbing)
   Is someone who buys something? (customer)
   Means to be excited and afraid? (panicking)
   Means something terrible? (dreadful)
   Is the opposite of funny? (serious)

   You may also review the courtroom glossary terms on page 1.

5. Introduce the story. Have students look at the title page. Students should read the title and the description on the title page.

   Retell what happened in the story so far. This is the second in the series of three books that tell the story of the Bobcat Cowboys on trial.

   Students will begin reading *Bobcat Cowboys On Trial* part 2. The chapter numbers continue from part 1. The chapters are numbered from 5 to 8 in this book.

6. Use the handwriting sheet or have the children write the following sentences:

   The opossum hid in the shrubs.
   The customer bought a sandwich.

LAR Answers

1. ○ small ○ swim ● huge
2. ● drive ○ gas ○ share
3. ● shape ○ green ○ circle
4. ○ mile ● inch ○ hour
5. ○ cry ○ snarl ● smile
6. ● letter ○ call ○ read
7. ○ graze ● green ○ grape
8. ○ feather ● tree ○ leaves

SAP Answers

Word List: orchard, shadow, together, sandwich, leather, whenever, theater, parachute, alphabet, sunshine, thanksgiving, whisper, shrub, paragraph, somewhere, Christmas

Sort the words by the vowel digraphs they contain.

ch: orchard, sandwich, parachute, Christmas

th: together, leather, theater, thanksgiving

sh: shadow, sunshine, shrub

wh: whenever, whisper, somewhere

ph: alphabet, paragraph

Unscramble the compound words. Write the spelling words.

answers in any order

somewhere thanksgiving whenever

Lesson 72

Lesson Objectives

1. Students will review the consonant digraphs. (P)
2. Students will review spelling words. (S)
3. Students will identify the subject and predicate parts of sentences. (L)
4. Students will read the story *Bobcat Cowboys On Trial* part 2. (R)
5. Students will copy sentences neatly and correctly. (H)
6. Students will write about word comparisons. (W)

Materials

LAR workbook page 71
SAP workbook page 62
WSW page 37
Book: *Bobcat Cowboys On Trial* part 2

Teaching

1. Use the top of the SAP workbook page. **Read the sentences. Some of the words have incorrect digraphs. Find and circle the misspelled words and write them correctly on the lines.**

2. Use the bottom section of the SAP workbook page and a blank piece of paper. Number the paper from 1 to 16. **The spelling words are written in code. Decode the words and write them on another piece of paper.**

3. **We have learned that sentences have different parts. What is the part that tells who or what the sentence is about?** (subject part) **What is the part that tells what it does?** (predicate) **Today you will complete sentences by adding a subject part or a predicate part.**

   Write part of a sentence: ________________ sat in a tree.

   Is the subject part or the predicate part missing in this sentence? (subject)

   Ask students to make up a subject part to complete the sentence.

   This sentence is missing the predicate part: The fuzzy bunny ____________.

   Ask students to complete the sentence by adding a predicate part.

   LAR workbook page 71: **Create the missing part of the sentences. What part did you write, the subject or predicate? Put an S in the box at the beginning of the sentence if you wrote a subject. Put a P in the box if you wrote the predicate.**

4. Ask the questions about chapter five of *Bobcat Cowboys On Trial* part 2. Then begin reading chapter six.

   Who were the last ones to find out that the Bobcats had escaped from jail? (the Bobcat Cowboys)
   Why didn't they know? (They the were looking for their trial, not trying to escape.)
   Where did the Bobcats go? (to a school) **Why?** (They thought that's where their trial was.)
   Who did they find there that they knew? (Miss Badger)
   How long had the bobcats been working on their math papers? (twenty years)
   Why did Bessybob go to the school? (The teacher called her.)
   What do you think will happen next?

5. Use the handwriting sheet or have the children write the following sentences:

   We saw a Christmas play at the theatre.
   Our whispering was disturbing the girl.

6. Students will compare the sets of words and tell how they are alike. Out of the seven sets, students will choose three to compare. The spelling and vocabulary list is provided for additional words students may use to describe the comparison.

   Taking some words from the previous week's words, following are some examples of comparing words for similarities.

   Magnify / shrink: Both words describe changing the size of something.

   Believe / Think: Both words use the brain to do.

   Butterflies / moths: Both are insects with large wings.

   Motorcycle / Bicycle: Both are things you ride with two wheels.

SAP Answers

1. telephone
2. everywhere
3. chimney
4. thought
5. should
6. with
7. elephant
8. chair

Code answers

1. together 2. theater 3. whenever
4. thanksgiving 5. Christmas
6. shadow 7. orchard 8. somewhere
9. paragraph 10. sandwich 11. shrub
12. whisper 13. parachute
14. sunshine 15. leather 16. alphabet

LAR Answers

Sentence completion answers vary.

1. S
2. P
3. P
4. S
5. S
6. P
7. S
8. P

Lesson 73

Lesson Objectives

1. Students will match subjects to predicates. (L)
2. Students will review vocabulary words. (L)
3. Students will review the spelling list. (S)
4. Students will read part of the story *Bobcat Cowboys On Trial* part 2. (R)
5. Students will copy sentences neatly and correctly. (H)
6. Students will compare differences between pairs of words. (W)

Materials

SAP workbook page 63
WSW page 38
Subject Predicate wheels (copy master)
Book: *Bobcat Cowboys On Trial* part 2

Teaching

1. Review the terms predicate and subject to describe parts of sentences. Cut out the subject and predicate wheels. The wheels don't connect other than touching edges. Have students set the wheels next to each other and read the sentence that is made where the two circles touch. (This will vary with different students.)

   Student can create a number of sentences by turning the wheels. Have students read and write some of the sentences. To extend the activity, students may create their own subject-predicate wheels. Blank wheels are provided in the copy master packet.

2. Review the vocabulary words. Students write sentences using the vocabulary words. You may dictate or have students copy the following sentences. Have students underline the vocabulary word:

   The <u>customer</u> bought a banana.
   The <u>opossum</u> climbed a tree.
   The baby's cries were <u>disturbing</u> my sleep.
   The judge was very <u>serious</u>.
   The rainy weather made the picnic <u>dreadful</u>.
   <u>Panicking</u> doesn't help.

   Discuss the meanings of the words.

3. Use the SAP workbook page. Top section: **Complete the words at the top of the page by adding consonant digraphs.**

   Bottom section: **Fill in the boxes to write spelling words in the grid. Start with the lines with clues** (letters).

4. Ask questions about chapter 6 of *Bobcat Cowboys On Trial* part 2. Then begin reading chapter 7.
Was Frazzle O'Hare trying to help defend the bobcats? (no)
How do you know? (He wanted the judge to lock them up and throw away the keys.)
What did he mean by "throw away the keys"? (Never let them out of jail.)
On page 10 what did Frazzle O'Hare mean by badgering the witness? (Picking on her or being mean to her.)
What were the bobcats accused of doing? (Disturbing the P's, Pizzas, and Pieces)
What do you think that means?

5. Use the handwriting sheet or have the children write the following sentences:

   The owl's nest is somewhere in the shadows.
   The family ate Thanksgiving dinner together.

6. This is like lesson 72 but focusing on differences. Students will compare the sets of words and tell how they are different. Out of the seven sets, students will choose three to compare. The spelling and vocabulary list is provided for additional words students may use to describe the comparison.

   Taking some words from the previous week's words, following are some examples of comparing words for differences.

   Everything / something: Something is part of everything.
   Movies / Plays: The actors are filmed in movies. The actors perform live in a play.
   Achieve / fail: If you achieve you are successful. If you fail, you are not successful.
   Windshield / Car: A windshield is only one part of a car.

SAP Answers

1. wheel 2. should 3. everywhere
4. photograph 5. church 6. think
7. marshmallow 8. pitcher
9. elephant 10. mother

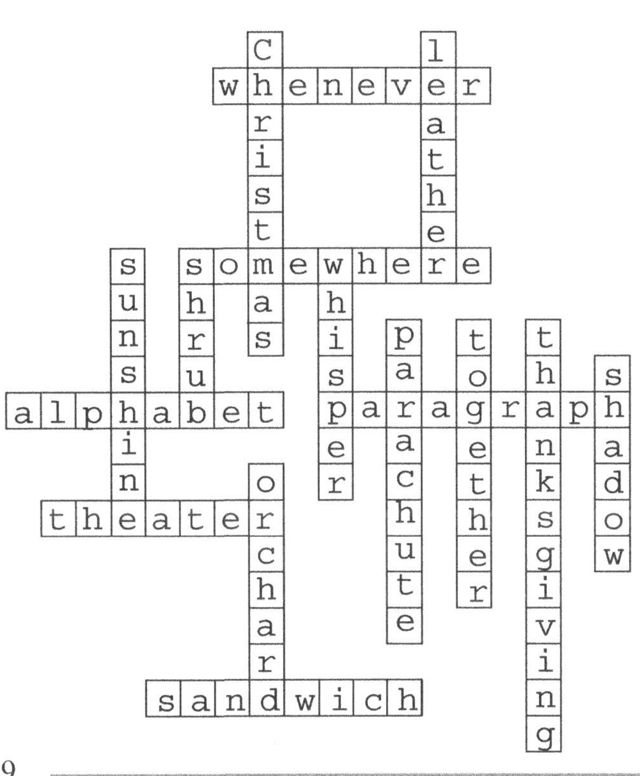

Lesson 74

Lesson Objectives

1. Students will review spelling words. (S)
2. Students will read the story *Bobcat Cowboys On Trial* part 2. (R)
3. Students will write a story. (CW)
4. Students will copy sentences neatly and correctly. (H)
5. Students will capitalize titles of books. (L)

Materials

SAP workbook page 64
Book: *Bobcat Cowboys On Trial* part 2
Resource Pack: Book title capitalization rules and lesson 74 practice sheet

Teaching

1. Use SAP workbook page 64. **Read the descriptions. Write the spelling words that match the descriptions.**

2. Ask questions about chapter 7.

   Who disturbed the pieces? (Billybob)
   What does that mean? (He added extra checkers to the checker board.)
   Why did Billybob do that? (He couldn't count correctly.)
   How do you know he couldn't count? (He added numbers and mixed some up.)
   What was Otto's dream? (He wanted to be Monday Night Checker Champ.)
   Why did the critters try to lose on Thursdays? (They didn't want to win stale crackers.)
   Why not?
   Do you think Billybob is guilty or innocent? Why?
   How do you think he should be punished?

   Students will now read chapter 8 of the book *Bobcat Cowboys On Trial* part 2.

3. Students should read chapter 8 before being introduced to the writing assignment.

   You are going out to eat at Peppy Possum's Pizza Parlor. Tell what it is like. You may bring your friends, pets, or your family. What kind of unusual pizza would you get? What other fun things are there to do at Peppy's?

4. Use the handwriting sheet or have the children write the following sentences:

   It would be dreadful to jump without a parachute.
   I would do some serious panicking.

5. Use the book title capitalization sheet as rules for capitalizing book titles are introduced. These are the rules for capitalizing titles of books, magazines, poems, movies, newspapers, stories, paintings, and other artistic works. Following is a review of the rules.

Less significant words are only capitalized if they are the first or last word of a title:

articles: a, an, the
prepositions less than 5 letters such as: in, on, of, to
conjunctions less than 5 letters such as: and, but, or, for
A word after a colon in a title is capitalized. The Bobcat Cowboys: A Cat Tale

Other short words are capitalized, for example:
Verbs: was, are, were, be.
Pronouns: my, he, his, she

Have students capitalize the titles on the lesson 74 book title capitalization practice sheet.

These are titles of actual books. McRuffy Press has not reviewed all the books and although the list may contain many quality books, McRuffy Press is not necessarily endorsing them.

SAP Answers

Use the clues to find the spelling words. A list is in the orange box.

orchard shadow together sandwich leather whenever parachute alphabet sunshine thanksgiving whisper theater shrub paragraph somewhere Christmas

December 25
Christmas

Lots of this if it is not cloudy
sunshine

parachute

Blocked sunlight
shadow

alphabet

paragraph

A place
somewhere

Cow hide
leather

Lots of apple trees
orchard

together

Speak quietly
whisper

whenever

A small tree
shrub

Hamburger
sandwich

To show gratefulness
thanksgiving

theater

Practice Sheet Answers

The Boy in Striped Pajamas
Everything on a Waffle
The Princess and the Goblin
The Cheshire Cat: A Dickens of a Tale
Binky to the Rescue
On the Banks of Plum Creek
Casey at the Bat
Falling Up

Lesson 75

Lesson Objectives

1. Students will answer questions about the story *Bobcat Cowboys On Trial* part 2. (L)
2. Students will take a spelling test. (S)
3. Students will compare and contrast animals. (L)
4. Students will read the stories they have written. (R)
5. Students will copy a sentence neatly and correctly. (H)

Materials

Creative writing assignment
Book: *Bobcat Cowboys On Trial* part 2
LAR Workbook pages 72, 73, and 74.

Teaching

1. Use LAR workbook page 72. **Answer the questions about the story, Bobcat Cowboys On Trial. Answers should be complete sentences.**

2. Have students number their paper from 1 to 14. Give the following words as dictation.

   1. whisper, 2. together, 3. shadow, 4. alphabet, 5. theater, 6. shrub, 7. Christmas, 8. leather, 9. somewhere, 10. sandwich, 11. whenever, 12. parachute, 13. orchard, 14. paragraph, 15. thanksgiving, 16. sunshine

3. Use LAR workbook pages 73 and 74. **Read the articles about bobcats and wolves on page 73. On page 74, answer the questions that compare and contrast the two animals. Fill in the circle that answers the question: bobcats, wolves, or both.**

Lesson 75

Text from workbook page 73

Read about the animals. Answer the questions on the next page.

Bobcats

Bobcats are a member of the cat family. They are called bobcats because they have short tails. Bobcats have spotted and striped fur coats. The fur is gray, tan or brown. The fur on their bellies is white. They have large paws and sharp claws.

A female bobcat will have a litter of two to four kittens. They may weigh four to eight ounces. Bobcats grow up to weigh twenty to thirty pounds. They are about thirty inches long.

Bobcats are good hunters. Their favorite food is rabbits or hares. They also eat other small rodents and birds. Sometimes bobcats will hunt larger animals such as deer and lambs. Most adult bobcats hunt and live by themselves.

Wolves

Wolves are related to dogs. They have long bushy tails. Wolves have thick fur. The color of the fur may be gray, white or reddish. They have large paws with fur between their toes.

A female wolf will have a litter of four to seven pups. They grow to weigh between sixty and one hundred twenty pounds. Gray wolves are about eighty inches long. Red wolves are smaller.

Wolves hunt in packs. A pack is a group of wolves that live together. They hunt large animals such as deer, moose, and antelope. They also eat small rodents, birds, insects, and even berries.

4. Have students read stories from the lesson 74 creative writing assignment.

5. Use the handwriting sheet or have the children write the following sentences:

   There are twenty-six letters in the alphabet.
   The leather pouch was filled with apples from the orchard.

LAR Page 72 Answers

Answers will vary.
Sample answers:

1. They didn't finish their math homework.
2. Bubba said they were the kind of cats that didn't eat rabbits.
3. They were replacing the lamps in the checker hall.
4. He was the owner of the pizza parlor.
5. He thought three times four was fourteen.

LAR Page 74 Answers

1. ● bobcats ○ wolves ○ both
2. ○ bobcats ○ wolves ● both
3. ● bobcats ○ wolves ○ both
4. ○ bobcats ● wolves ○ both
5. ○ bobcats ○ wolves ● both
6. ○ bobcats ● wolves ○ both
7. ● bobcats ○ wolves ○ both
8. ○ bobcats ○ wolves ● both
9. ○ bobcats ● wolves ○ both
10. ○ bobcats ○ wolves ● both

Lesson 76

Students will use Lessons 76 to 79 to prepare for the mid-year test. Concepts will be reviewed. A reading book is assigned only for Lessons 76-78. The test will be given during Lesson 80. Students will be tested over language concepts, vocabulary development, reading comprehension, and spelling.

Lesson Objectives

1. Students will review vocabulary words. (L)
2. Students will review prefixes. (L)
3. Students will spell words correctly. (S)
4. Students will read the story *Bobcat Cowboys On Trial* part 3
5. Students will copy sentences neatly and correctly. (H)

Materials

LAR workbook page 75
SAP workbook page 65
Bobcat Cowboys On Trial part 3

Teaching

1. The following words were chosen from the vocabulary lists for each book.

   Words for *Bobcat Cowboys on Trial* part 3: **allergic, business, concerned, handsome, mathematical, theatre**

   Review List: **imaginary, creature, explain, dangerous, porcupine, serious**

   Have students copy the list. Use part 1 of LAR page 75. Have students answer the questions using vocabulary words.

2. Write the prefixes un, re, and pre. Review the term, prefix. Ask students what is the term for letters such as un, re, and pre that are added to the beginning of words. (prefix) Each of these prefixes have meanings in many words.

   How are the words happy and unhappy different? (They're opposites) **What does unhappy mean?** (not happy)

   Re means to go back to the way things were – replace, or to repeat an action – retest. What does redo mean? (do again)

   Pre means before. If you prepare dinner, you are making the food before you eat it. What is a pretest? (a practice test you take before the final test)

   Write the words school, kind, and try. Ask students to choose one of the prefixes for each word to make the new words. Ask students to define the new words.

   Use part 2 of LAR page 75. Students will add the correct prefix: pre, re, un to each word to complete the definition.

3. Use the SAP workbook page. **Read the words in the pink box. This is a review list made up of words from past spelling lessons. Alphabetize the two groups of words.**

   Spelling List: adventure, rectangle, continue, nephew, shoestring, mountain, eyebrow, breakfast, teacher, approach, toaster, rejoice, avoid, windshield, butterflies, country, parachute, whisper, alphabet, shadow

   This is the spelling list for the spelling test given in Lesson 80. Students will use this list to prepare for the test.

4. Ask students to retell the events of the trial so far. Have students read the new vocabulary words on the title page of the book. Students should then read the description on the title page of the book. Ask students to make predictions on what Bubba is accused of doing and do they think he really did disturb the p's, and what is Disturbing the P's?

5. Use the handwriting sheet or have the children write the following sentences:

   The teacher wrote the alphabet on a chalkboard.
   An untied shoestring can be dangerous.

LAR Answers

Part 1

1. porcupine
2. creature
3. theater
4. mathematical
5. business
6. serious
7. imaginary
8. explain
9. handsome
10. concerned
11. dangerous
12. allergic

Part 2

1. pre
2. re
3. un
4. re
5. un
6. pre
7. un
8. re
9. pre
10. re

SAP Answers

1. adventure
2. alphabet
3. approach
4. avoid
5. breakfast
6. butterflies
7. continue
8. country
9. eyebrow

1. mountain
2. nephew
3. parachute
4. rectangle
5. rejoice
6. shadow
7. shoestring
8. teacher
9. toaster
10. whisper
11. windshield

Lesson 77

Lesson Objectives

1. Students will review and determine parts of speech by context (nouns and verbs). (L)
2. Students will review tense (present, past, future). (L)
3. Students will review subject and predicate parts of sentences. (L)
4. Students will review spelling words. (S)
5. Students will read the story *Bobcat Cowboys On Trial* part 3 (R)
6. Students will copy sentences neatly and correctly. (H)
7. Students will research different alphabets. (W)

Materials

LAR workbook page 76
SAP workbook page 66
WSW 39
Bobcat Cowboys On Trial part 3

Teaching

1. Write the word, stand. Ask the students to define the terms noun and verb. Noun: person, place, thing. Verb: tells what a noun does.

   Is the word, stand, a noun or a verb? (Students may give an answer, but until the word is applied in context, we don't know.)

   Read these sentences to the students and ask if stand was a noun or verb in each one.

   Bubba owned a marshmallow hamburger *stand*. (noun)
   Alice McHoot will *stand* in line to buy a marshmallow hamburger. (verb)

   Some words can be nouns or verbs depending on how they are used in the sentence.

   LAR workbook page 76 part 1: **Fill in the oval that tells how the word in bold print is used.**

2. Review present, past, and future tense. Have students find the verbs and tell the tense in the following sentences:

   The judge pounded his gavel. (past)
   Bobbybill is robbing the stagecoach. (present)
   Bubba will solve math problems. (future)

   Use part 2 of LAR workbook page 76. **Read the sentences. Find the verb. Is the verb past, present or future tense? Fill in the correct circle.**

3. Review subject and predicate parts of sentences. **What is the subject part of a sentence?** (It tells who or what is doing the action.) **What is the predicate?** (It is the part that tells what the subject is doing.)

   Use the example: **The red squirrel climbed the old oak tree. What is the subject part of the sentence?** (the red squirrel) **The predicate tells what the subject does. What is the predicate?** (climbed the old oak tree)

   Students will use parts 1 and 2 of LAR workbook page 76. In part 1, have students underline the subject parts of each of the sentences. In part 2, have students underline the predicate parts of the sentences.

4. Use the SAP page. Top section: **Decode spelling words by using the number problems. Start on the letter on the top of each problem. Move right the number of places if you are adding. Move left if you are subtracting. Let's look at the first problem, n + 2. Start at the letter n on the number line and move two places to the right. What letter solves the problem?** (p) Continue with the next problem, d - 3. **Start at the d. Subtract 3, so move to the left three letters.What letter do you end at?** (a)

   On the second section, write compound words and the corresponding numbers for their parts. For example the parts 1 and 4 make the word *breakfast*. Write the word breakfast next on the lines next to 1,4.

5. Ask questions about chapter 9.
   What kind of business did Miss Fussybunny have? (a puppet stand)
   What happened to it? (Bubba burned it down.)
   How did Bubba disturb the p's? (He change the name Buppa to Bubba.)
   Do you think Bubba meant to be bad?
   Should Bubba be punished? If so, how?
   What do you think Frazzle meant when he said "I'll take care of that"?

   Students will now read chapter 10 of the book *Bobcat Cowboys On Trial* part 3.

6. Use the handwriting sheet or have the children write the following sentences:
   Climbing a mountain would be an adventure. We cooked our breakfast in the toaster.

7. Students will research to find different alphabets of the world. Students will write the names of the alphabets and draw some examples of different letters in the boxes. If possible, have students try to phonetically write common English words with the alphabet, such as cat. Students would write the equivalent of the k, short a, and t sounds, although students should be made aware that the actual language may have a very different word for cat.

LAR Answers

1. ● noun ❍ verb
2. ❍ noun ● verb
3. ❍ noun ● verb
4. ● noun ❍ verb
5. ● noun ❍ verb
6. ❍ noun ● verb
7. ● noun ❍ verb
8. ❍ noun ● verb
9. ❍ noun ● verb
10. ● noun ❍ verb

1. ● past ❍ present ❍ future
2. ❍ past ❍ present ● future
3. ❍ past ● present ❍ future
4. ● past ❍ present ❍ future
5. ❍ past ❍ present ● future
6. ● past ❍ present ❍ future
7 ❍ past ● present ❍ future
8. ❍ past ● present ❍ future
9. ● past ❍ present ❍ future
10. ❍ past ❍ present ● future

SAP Answers

Part 1

parachute nephew

country avoid shadow
rectangle teacher

adventure mountain

Part 2 answers can be in any order:

1,4 breakfast

5,2 shoestring

9,6 butterflies

7,10 eyebrow

3,8 windshield

Lesson 78

Lesson Objectives

1. Students will review categorizing words. (L)
2. Students will review analogies. (L)
3. Students will review the spelling list. (S)
4. Students will read the story *Bobcat Cowboys On Trial* part 3 (R)
5. Students will copy sentences neatly and correctly. (H)
6. Students will use a form to create detailed sentences. (W)

Materials

LAR workbook page 77
SAP workbook page 67
WSW pages 40 and 41
Bobcat Cowboys On Trial part 3

Teaching

1. Write the words toaster, oven, skillet. **How are the meanings of these words alike?** (You cook with all of them.)

   Use part 1 of LAR workbook page 77. **Descriptions of groups of words have a letter next to each of them. Write the letter on the blank that describes the group of words.**

2. Review analogies. **An analogy is when we compare the relationship to one pair of words to another pair of words.**

   Hot is to cold as bright is to ______. (dark)

   Use part 2 of LAR workbook page 77. **Complete the analogies. Fill in the correct circle.**

3. Use SAP page 67. **Fill in the blank lines on the page using spelling words. In the top section, you will complete the sentences using the words in the top box.**

   Bottom section: **Match the clues to the words in the bottom box.**

4. Ask questions about chapter 10 and then have students read chapter 11.

   What important question did Frazzle ask Miss Fussybunny? (He asked her to marry him.)
   Do you think he knew her before the trial began? (Yes) **What makes you think so?**
   Why wasn't the jury allowed to hug Frazzle? (They wanted to eat him.)
   What did the critters think the judge meant when he sentenced Frazzle to life?
   (He would have to go to jail for the rest of his life.)
   What did the judge really mean? (Frazzle would live the rest of his life with Harriet.)
   How long did it take the jury to decide if the bobcats were guilty? (two minutes)
   Why do you think it took such a short amount of time?
   What do you think is going to happen to the bobcats?

5. Use the handwriting sheet or have the children write the following sentences:

   The butterflies landed on my nephew's eyebrow.
   The crowd rejoiced when the parachute opened.

Lesson 78

6. This lesson encourages students to add phrases and words to expand the amount of information in a sentence. Using spelling or vocabulary words as key words, students will add details that answer questions. The spelling or vocabulary word can be a part of any box. The first page is an example of how to fill in the boxes. The second page is provided so students can create their own detailed sentences. The entries in each box should flow to create a sentence. On the example page two sentences were created.

   The red ball bounced off the windshield after I kicked it because I missed the goal. The silly boy made shadow puppets on the wall at the party to make us laugh.

   But, those aren't the only sentences that can be made. Students should experiment by reading or writing the parts in a different order. For example:

   Because I missed the goal, the red ball bounced off the windshield after I kicked it.

   Students may also switch parts between sentences. The results can be nonsensical or logical. For example: The red ball made shadow puppets off the windshield at the party to make us laugh. At the party, the red ball bounced on the wall because I missed the goal.

   Students can include parts of the sentences they create to make silly or logical sentences. Have students choose parts from each question detail.

   Subject: this box includes the subject. Encourage students to add adjectives that describe the subject.

   Action: it can be a simple verb or more details like the shadow example.

   Where: this will generally be a prepositional phrase.

   When: it can be a definite time such as yesterday or at 4:30. It can also indicate order such as the windshield example. The shadow example indicates during an event.

   Why: a statement of a reason for the action.

LAR Answers

Part 1

1. C
2. F
3. H
4. B
5. J
6. I
7. D
8. A
9. G
10. E

Part 2

1.	❍ small	● swim	❍ and
2.	❍ mother	❍ cousin	● aunt
3.	● dog	❍ muskrat	❍ cowboy
4.	❍ nose	❍ foot	● hand
5.	● sad	❍ glad	❍ sleep
6.	❍ go	● avoid	❍ run
7.	● soft	❍ quills	❍ carrot
8.	❍ warm	● cold	❍ burn
9.	❍ fake	❍ antlers	● real
10.	❍ prepare	❍ unfill	● fill

SAP Answers

Part 1

teacher whisper
toaster breakfast
windshield rectangle
mountain adventure
butterflies country

Part 2

eyebrow
nephew alphabet
approach
rejoice
shoestring shadow
continue parachute
avoid

Lesson 79

Lesson Objectives

1. Students will review comprehension skills. (L)
2. Students will review vocabulary words. (L)
3. Students will review spelling words. (S)
4. Students will answer questions about the story *Bobcat Cowboys On Trial* part 3
5. Students will copy sentences neatly and correctly. (H)

Materials

LAR workbook pages 78
SAP workbook page 68
Bobcat Cowboys On Trial part 3

Teaching

1. Use LAR workbook page 78 part 1. Students will read the story and answer the questions. Review the term main idea. **The main idea of a paragraph is a sentence that best tells what the whole paragraph is about.** Students will be asked to write the main idea of the paragraph.

   Students will also answer four other questions. One of which will be an inference question. This will require students to make an assumption or inference based on the information in the paragraph.

2. Use LAR workbook page 78 part 2. Students will choose the vocabulary words that complete the sentences.

3. Use SAP workbook page 68. **Match the spelling words to the descriptions. Write the words on the lines.**

4. Have students answer the questions about Chapter 11 and read the rest of the story, *Bobcat Cowboys on Trial* part 3.

   What or how did each bobcat hang? (Billybob hung lanterns. Bobbybill hung upside down as he washed pizza pans. Bubba hung curtains.)
   What other punishment did the bobcats get? (They couldn't be in the horseshoe tossing contest and they had to do some hard times in the pen.)
   What was meant by "hard times in the pen"? (They had to do multiplication problems in the hog pen.)
   Do you think the bobcats learned their lesson?
   Do you think Frazzle O'Hare will work harder to defend the bobcats if he needs to in the future? What makes you think that?
   Do you think they'll cause problems in Rodent Gulch in the future?
   Did you like this story? What did you like the most? (or least?)

5. Use the handwriting sheet or have the children write the following sentences:

   Mr. O'Hare continued to avoid the jury.
   A windshield is a shaped like a rectangle.

LAR Answers

Part 1

Wording may vary

1. This was a terrible day to move.
2. They ran out of tape.
3. Rainy. They covered the furniture so it wouldn't get wet.
4. The big truck was late.

Part 2

Added word is in bold. Additional word is underlined.

1. The **porcupine** is a <u>creature</u> with quills.
2. We saw a play at the **theater** about an <u>imaginary</u> rabbit.
3. You need to solve **mathematical** problems to have a successful <u>business</u>.
4. We were very **concerned** about the <u>dangerous</u> roads.
5. Being <u>allergic</u> to pets can be a **serious** problem for a vet.

What two words were not used? (handsome, explain)

SAP Answers

Use the clues to find the spelling words. A list is in the orange box.

adventure rectangle continue nephew shoestring mountain
eyebrow breakfast teacher approach toaster rejoice avoid
windshield butterflies country parachute whisper alphabet shadow

A boy relative

nephew

Use this to spell

alphabet

approach

It heats food.

toaster

To be happy

rejoice

To speak quietly

whisper

To keep going

continue

Hair on a face

eyebrow

Not in a city, lots of fields

country

Learn from this person

teacher

They begin as caterpillars.

butterflies

A shape with four sides

rectangle

Tall, rocky, land

mountain

Stay away

avoid

It needs a wiper.

windshield

adventure

Lesson 80

Lesson Objectives

1. Students will take a test.

Materials

Test 2 Pages 1 to 4

Test Directions and Scoring

Boxes are provided at the end of each subtest. Multiplying the number of correct answers by the number given will yield a total of 100 points for the test, not counting the spelling test.

Word Structure Subtests:

Part 1: Add prefixes to the seven words. Choose from pre, re, or un. Write the new words on the lines.

***Scoring:** Each answer counts as 1 point for a total possible score of 7 points.*

Part 2: Answer the questions about prefixes by writing a prefix on the blank. (pre, re, or un)

***Scoring:** Each answer counts as 1 point for a total possible score of 3 points.*

Comprehension Subtest:

Part 3: Read the paragraph. Answer the questions.

***Scoring:** Multiply the number correct by 4 for a total possible score of 20 points.*

Grammar Subtests:

Part 4: Read the sentences. Underline the subject part. Circle the predicate part.

***Scoring:** Multiply total correct of all three parts by 2 for a total possible score of 10 points.*

Part 5: Read the sentences. The verbs are in bold print. Fill in the circle that tells the tense of the verbs.

***Scoring:** Multiply total correct of all three parts by 2 for a total possible score of 10 points.*

Part 6: Read the sentences. A word that could be a noun or a verb is in bold print. The context of the sentence will tell how it is used. Is it a noun or verb? Fill in the correct circle.

***Scoring:** Multiply total correct of all three parts by 2 for a total possible score of 10 points.*

Vocabulary Subtests:

Part 7: Answer the question using a vocabulary word.

***Scoring:** Multiply the total correct of both parts by 2 for a total possible score of 10 points.*

Part 8: Choose the best vocabulary word to complete each sentence.

***Scoring:** Multiply the total correct of both parts by 2 for a total possible score of 10 points.*

Language Subtest:

Part 9: Complete the analogy. Fill in the circle next to the best choice.

***Scoring:** Multiply the total correct of both parts by 2 for a total possible score of 10 points.*

Part 10: Tell how the words in each group are alike. Match the letter at the beginning of the descriptions to tell how the words are alike. One description will not be used.

***Scoring:** Multiply the total correct of both parts by 2 for a total possible score of 10 points.*

Spelling Test: Fill in the circle next to the correctly spelled words. Answers (also on answer sheet)

1. shadow, 2. avoid, 3. rectangle, 4. breakfast, 5. continue, 6. teacher, 7. toaster, 8. mountain, 9. windshield, 10. alphabet, 11. country, 12. eyebrow, 13. butterflies, 14. adventure, 15. approach, 16. shoestring, 17. parachute, 18. rejoice, 19. whisper, 20. nephew

***Scoring:** Multiply the total correct by five for a total possible score of 100 points.*

Page 1

Part 1 Add prefixes to the words. Choose from pre, re, or un. Write the prefixes on the lines before the words.

1. _____move 2. _____known 3. _____wind
4. _____safe
5. _____historic 6. _____thankful 7. _____school

Part 2 Write the prefix that matches the definition:

8. _____ To do ahead of time.

9. _____ To do again.

10. _____ To do the opposite.

Part 3: Read the paragraph. Answer the questions.

Everything is new this season. I have a brand new glove and bat. Coach Rick is coaching his first team. I like my new blue uniform. I don't know any of the other players. My mother says I'll have fun making new friends. I think she is right!

1. What is the main idea of the paragraph?
____
____

2. What sport is the person going to play? _______________________

3. Who is the coach of the team? _____________________________

4. What color was the uniform?_____________________________

5. What does the mother say about the season?_____________________
____

Page 2

Part 7 Answer the questions using vocabulary words from the list.

Vocabulary word list for parts 7 and 8:

allergic, business, concerned, creature, dangerous, explain, handsome, imaginary, mathematical, porcupine, serious, theatre

1. Not safe _______________

2. Nice looking _____________

3. To tell how something works ____________________

4. Not real _________________

5. Not funny _________________

Part 8 Complete the sentences using vocabulary words from the list in part 7.

1. The boy was sneezing because he was ____________________ to cats.

2. The ____________________ was protected by its quills.

3. We watched a movie at the ____________________.

4. The book was full of ______________________ problems to solve.

5. We were very ____________________ about the high winds and dark clouds.

Page 3

Part 9 Complete the analogies. Fill in the circle next to the best answer.

1. Hot is to cold as safe is to	❍ warm	❍ secure	❍ dangerous
2. Cat is to fur as chicken is to	❍ egg	❍ feathers	❍ dog
3. Waffle is to square as pancake is to	❍ circle	❍ syrup	❍ breakfast
4. Bell is to sound as fire is to	❍ heat	❍ ring	❍ ice
5. Pillow is to hard as tired is to	❍ sleep	❍ rested	❍ bed

Part 10 Read the groups of words. Write the letter at the beginning of the descriptions to tell how the words are alike. One description will not be used.

1. _____paper, pizza, bad tires
2. _____computers, pianos, locks
3. _____clouds, balloons, ships
4. _____tape, candy, glue
5. _____bulls, trucks, orchestra

A. Things that are sticky
B. Things that are flat.
C. Things that have horns.
D. Things that are round.
E. Things that have keys.
F. Things that float.

Spelling Test: Fill in the circle next to the correct spelling of the word.

1.	❍ shaddow	❍ shadoe	❍ shadow	❍ chadow	11. ❍ kountry	❍ country	❍ contree	❍ countrie
2.	❍ avoid	❍ aviod	❍ avode	❍ uvoide	12. ❍ iebrou	❍ eiebrou	❍ ibrow	❍ eyebrow
3.	❍ recktangle	❍ rectangel	❍ wrectangle	❍ rectangle	13. ❍ butterflys	❍ butterflies	❍ buterflizes	❍ buttorflies
4.	❍ breakfast	❍ breakfest	❍ breckfist	❍ brekfust	14. ❍ adventure	❍ abventure	❍ addventure	❍ advenshure
5.	❍ continew	❍ continue	❍ cuntinoo	❍ contenue	15. ❍ aproach	❍ aproash	❍ approach	❍ approtch
6.	❍ teecher	❍ teasher	❍ teacher	❍ theacher	16. ❍ shoestring	❍ shoestrig	❍ schoesting	❍ shoostring
7.	❍ toester	❍ toaster	❍ toastor	❍ tosetur	17. ❍ quarashute	❍ quarachute	❍ parashute	❍ parachute
8.	❍ mountin	❍ montain	❍ mountain	❍ mownten	18. ❍ rejoise	❍ rejoice	❍ rejuice	❍ rejoyce
9.	❍ windshield	❍ windshild	❍ winshield	❍ whenshield	19. ❍ wisper	❍ wishper	❍ whisper	❍ whispre
10.	❍ alfabet	❍ alphabet	❍ aphabet	❍ owlphabit	20. ❍ nefoe	❍ nephew	❍ knephew	❍ nehpew

Test 2 Answers

Part 1

1. remove 2. unknown 3. rewind 4. unsafe
5. prehistoric 6. unthankful 7. preschool

Part 2

1. pre
2. re
3. un

Part 3

1. Everything is new this season.
2. baseball
3. Coach Rick
4. Blue
5. I'll have fun making friends. (wording may vary)

Part 4

1. The big yellow cat hissed at the barking dog.
2. The ball bounced onto the road.
3. The new song was a hit.
4. The bright morning sun rose above the campground.
5. The yellow bus turned around in our driveway.

Part 5

1.	❍ past	● present	❍ future
2.	❍ past	❍ present	● future
3.	● past	❍ present	❍ future
4.	● past	❍ present	❍ future
5.	❍ past	❍ present	● future

Part 6

1.	❍ noun	● verb
2.	● noun	❍ verb
3.	● noun	❍ verb
4.	● noun	❍ verb
5.	❍ noun	● verb

Part 7

1. dangerous
2. handsome
3. explain
4. imaginary
5. serious

Part 8

1. allergic
2. porcupine
3. theater
4. mathematical
5. concerned

Part 9

1.	❍ warm	❍ secure	● dangerous
2.	❍ egg	● feathers	❍ dog
3.	● circle	❍ syrup	❍ breakfast
4.	● heat	❍ ring	❍ ice
5.	❍ sleep	● rested	❍ bed

Part 10

1. B
2. E
3. F
4. A
5. C

Spelling Test

1.	❍ shaddow	❍ shadoe	● shadow	❍ chadow	11.	❍ kountry	● country	❍ contree	❍ countrie
2.	● avoid	❍ aviod	❍ avode	❍ uvoide	12.	❍ iebrou	❍ eiebrou	❍ ibrow	● eyebrow
3.	❍ recktangle	❍ rectangel	❍ wrectangle	● rectangle	13.	❍ butterflys	● butterflies	❍ buterflizes	❍ buttorflies
4.	● breakfast	❍ breakfest	❍ breckfist	❍ brekfust	14.	● adventure	❍ abventure	❍ addventure	❍ advenshure
5.	❍ continew	● continue	❍ cuntinoo	❍ contenue	15.	❍ aproach	❍ aproash	● approach	❍ approtch
6.	❍ teecher	❍ teasher	● teacher	❍ theacher	16.	● shoestring	❍ shoestrig	❍ schoesting	❍ shoostring
7.	❍ toester	❍ toaster	● toastor	❍ tosetur	17.	❍ quarashute	❍ quarachute	❍ parashute	● parachute
8.	❍ mountin	❍ montain	● mountain	❍ mownten	18.	❍ rejoise	● rejoice	❍ rejuice	❍ rejoyce
9.	● windshield	❍ windshild	❍ winshield	❍ whenshield	19.	❍ wisper	❍ wishper	● whisper	❍ whispre
10.	❍ alfabet	● alphabet	❍ aphabet	❍ owlphabit	20.	❍ nefoe	● nephew	❍ knephew	❍ nehpew

Made in the USA
Monee, IL
14 June 2025